BOOK NOW!

INTERNET MARKETING
—FOR—
HEALTHCARE PRACTICES

GARRETT SMITH

Printed in the United States of America.

First printing, 2018.
Distributed by Pitch + Pivot, LLC

ISBN 978-0-692-99786-4

Book design by Reann Nye
www.reannnye.rocks

TABLE OF CONTENTS

INTRODUCTION

The internet has changed the patient-doctor landscape forever.

It wasn't very long ago that acquiring and maintaining a base of patients was a straightforward matter for a health care provider: as long as he or she provided excellent medical service, his or her patient base would grow. Between the phone book and word-of-mouth referrals from family, friends, and other medical professionals, a good practitioner could maintain steady patient growth without having to actively market his or her practice.

That has changed in recent years. The people who make up your current and future patient base are now online, and the information they're accessing on their computers, tablets, and smartphones is influencing their decisions just as much as recommendations from their family and friends.

> Searching for health-related information is currently the third most popular online activity, and more than half of adults in the United States use the internet as their first source for answers to their medical questions.

Patients have access to more data, more statistics, more tools, and more choices than ever before. Bombarded with information (or worse, misinformation) and overwhelmed with options, standing out to patients requires the modern medical practitioner to break free from the old way of thinking that said, "Practice great medicine and the business will take care of itself."

To thrive in the age of the internet, you must practice both great medicine and great marketing.

I

By the time you've finished reading this book, you will know how to resolve the following challenges, which are becoming increasingly detrimental to today's health and medical practices:

- Practice webpages that don't attract new patients or meet the needs of your existing patients
- Search engine results derived from online authority, rather than medical expertise
- Inaccurate medical listings and inconsistent practice data on internet directories and maps
- Misleading review websites that don't reflect the offline reality
- Lack of patient engagement with blogging and social media

If you're not sure where to start when it comes to improving your online footprint, the following twelve chapters will provide you with insight and actionable checklists to follow, all designed to help facilitate the successful marketing of your practice online, using modern methodologies and proven processes that have already helped dozens of practices around the world.

My name is Garrett Smith. I was an early practitioner of internet marketing, leading marketing efforts for a New York-based VoIP (Voice over Internet Protocol) company that grew from $2.5 million in revenue in 2004 to over $25 million in revenue by 2013, gaining the company a 100,000 monthly website visitors and over 100,000 worldwide customers in the process.

I stumbled into the healthcare industry by chance in 2010. A friend introduced me to a friend that had recently taken over the management of his father's New York City dermatology practice. They needed help enhancing their internet presence, and launching their skin care line via an ecommerce website.

I figured I could help them. I took the playbook I had developed and redesigned it to take advantage of the opportunities I saw online for healthcare practices. Forward seven years. We are still working together.

This first engagement lead to one referral after another. One of the nation's top orthopedic surgeons, then a new dental practice, followed by the team chiropractor for a pro sports team, and a celebrity dermatologist. A small group sports medicine practice grew into working with a large group physical therapy practice. Then came hospitals, after one of my first clients was acquired, and refused to stop working with us.

For the last seven years, applying my extensive background in internet marketing has resulted in thousands of patient visits to client's practices across the country. I have even had the opportunity to be part of the team launching a new product for a billion dollar biopharmaceutical company. These experiences have led to the creation of this book, a company, and a suite of services and software that assists practices in taking advantage of the power of internet marketing.

InboundMD, the company I founded, helps practitioners thrive in today's changing and challenging business landscape. InboundMD provides an all-in-one marketing solution that allows you to acquire new patients, protect your reputation, and publish social content, all without having to be a marketing expert. We serve as your marketing department and treat your practice as a business, allowing you to focus solely on treating your patients.

This book will discuss many of the proven internet marketing methodologies and techniques we've used, allowing you to begin implementing them for your practice. If you would like further information on any particular topic or would like to discuss something with one of our seasoned marketing professionals, please don't hesitate to contact us at 1-800-818-7199, email garrett@InboundMD.com, or visit www.InboundMD.com.

Without any further ado then, let's get started!

CHAPTER 1

GETTING STARTED WITH INTERNET MARKETING

Before we begin discussing the best ways to market your practice online, it might be helpful to take a brief moment to explain exactly what internet marketing is.

Internet marketing seeks to influence how consumers discover, research, evaluate, and eventually decide upon a provider from which to purchase goods and services via the internet. It's similar to the general field of marketing in scope, with the exception that internet marketing is based on pull rather than push methodologies; while traditional marketing involves pushing out your message, online marketing requires you to reach customers (in your case, patients) by pulling them in to your website or office via a number of inbound channels.

Some of these major internet marketing channels include:

- Search engines, such as Google and Bing
- Doctor review websites, among them Healthgrades and Vitals
- Blogs, especially those written by local individuals
- Social networks, including Facebook and Instagram

Since there are so many different channels available for marketing your health care practice, there are also a number of different ways to take advantage of them. The most popular strategies and tactics include search engine optimization (SEO), content marketing (blogging), reputation management, pay-per-click (PPC) advertising, and social media marketing.

Each of these internet marketing strategies plays a role in the patient journey – from initially finding a health care provider, to evaluating the provider against other similar providers, and finally to how the patient ultimately decides upon which provider to go to for care.

Don't worry if this all seems like too much – each strategy is explained in further detail in later chapters. For now, rather than delving deeply into the ins and outs of internet marketing, let's instead take a look at the advantages that come with it.

ADVANTAGES OF INTERNET MARKETING FOR HEALTH CARE PRACTICES

There are numerous advantages for health care practices when it comes to internet marketing, especially when compared to their traditional marketing counterparts.

These advantages include:
- **Cost**-Unlike traditional marketing channels, internet marketing is relatively inexpensive. Since the cost of delivering content online (text, video, etc.) is less than in the physical, offline world, health care providers can effectively grow awareness for their practice with even modest budgets.
- **Engagement**- The internet allows patients to interact directly with providers through content, blogs, videos, and social networks. Even the ads themselves can be interactive-patients love polls, surveys, and multiple choice questions. *Remember: the best marketing doesn't look like marketing at all.*
- **Targeting**-The internet allows you to get very specific with your marketing, targeting specific patients you want to reach with advanced activity, demographic, and life-event settings. These targeting features allow many health care practices to reach groups of patients they could have never effectively reached before.
- **Measurement**-Virtually everything on the internet is trackable. Yes, this can occasionally be taken too far and border on creepy, but for a health care practice it means that marketing campaigns can be operated and measured based on established metrics of success. This gives you the data that will ensure that you stay within your target cost per new patient acquired.
- **Time**-Since there are so few barriers to entry on the internet, creating and launching an online marketing campaign is less time and resource-intense than doing so through traditional channels.

In addition to these benefits of online marketing, it's also important to realize that internet marketing represents a bit of a paradigm shift as it relates to marketing in general. To expand on that point further, let's examine the advantages of internet marketing another way – exploring the differences between push and pull marketing.

PUSH MARKETING

For decades, brands created something (a good or service) and then spent an enormous amount of time and money pushing this product through advertising channels on to the end consumer. This "push" is defined through a message (ad) directed at a consumer.

Since traditional communication channels were A) limited (TV, print, radio) and B) controlled (your cable provider dictates programming, for example), the messages delivered allowed for no interaction between brand and consumer. This created an environment in which the brand could control what consumers saw, heard, and thought about a particular product or service, but also one in which only the largest and most well-funded of brands could effectively reach enough of the population (the mass market) to sustain operations.

This meant that there was a limited amount of brands and products for consumers to choose from. It also made it hard for many health care providers to successfully market their practice, as the cost of advertising through newspapers, radio, and TV prohibited all but the largest practices from doing so.

PULL MARKETING

With the advent of the internet, a new medium was created that allowed consumers to find, evaluate, and decide which products to purchase in a manner not previously available. This meant that consumers –your patients– could dictate how and when they were exposed to different products and services. The internet also allowed for interaction to take place between brands and the end consumer.

As a result, *consumers have taken to the internet in droves as they've gained the ability to control–or at least take part in– the messaging that they're being shown.* This has given patients ever-increasing say in how they are being marketed to and has resulted in smart health care practices being present where their patients are online, creating messages that pull patients in.

A clear example of pull marketing for a health care practice is the creation of a well-optimized health care website, especially one that ranks highly on Google for its related search terms. In this example, if a patient decided to go to Google to search for information about an issue he or she may be having, he or she would click on one of the listings displayed in the search results. By doing so, he or she would be "pulled" to that particular web page.

Today, most internet marketing tactics and strategies are based on pulling a consumer/patient from a channel they use to find, evaluate, review, and/or compare information about a product or service back to one's offering. This is often referred to as inbound marketing.

Although push marketing was and is more prevalent with traditional marketing, some internet marketing techniques are also "push" in nature. Email newsletters and Facebook allow for brands to push content out to consumers, though the consumers must be subscribed in order to receive the communications. Consumers can respond directly to this content, as well – an interaction that newspapers, radio, and TV don't allow.

THE 4 P'S OF INTERNET MARKETING

Internet marketing still encompasses the four P's of traditional marketing – product, price, place and promotion. Each of these four core aspects has evolved, however, based on the workings of the internet and the new marketing channels that have emerged.

- **Product (People)**–For decades, traditional marketing started with a product, which was created and pushed upon the consumer. Today, product has become people – in other words, people, not brands, now dictate what is needed and how it is acquired.

- **Price (Purpose)**–Price has traditionally set the value of an item. It still does to some extent, but more important than price in setting value is purpose. Today, most buyers judge the value of a product or service based on its purpose.

- **Place (Position)**–The place–how you got your product to buyers –was the third pillar of marketing. Today, getting products and services to consumers is still a function, but more important than place is the position (search rank) of what is being marketed. This means being "present" where buyers are going to discover, evaluate, review, and compare potential products or services.

- **Promotion (Passion)**–The old world relied on promotions (discounts, sales, etc.) in order to drive sales of new and/or underperforming products and services. Today, a company's passion for what it sells determines whether or not a buyer will take notice. Passion is one of the most powerful of all human emotions, and it can't be manufactured. Passion not only rounds out the new 4 P's, but completes the circle back to people. When people get passionate about your products, services, and company, they can help promote and build your brand faster and stronger than you could on your own.

THE FIFTH P OF INTERNET MARKETING

The internet has also brought forth a fifth (and perhaps more important) P - performance.

Thanks to the internet, almost all marketing tactics and advertising campaigns can be tracked, in order to give you insight into their performance and efficacy. Through website analytics, specific campaign tracking links, and other technology, you can view every piece of a patient's interaction with your clinic - from the first time he or she clicked on an ad to the rating that was left on your profile after his or her visit.

These insights allow for metric-based marketing and make understanding your return on investment (ROI) more transparent than ever before. This in turn makes investing time and money into marketing your practice a safer bet, as you'll be able to see data on the strength of a particular campaign in real time. At worst, you'll know what strategies are not working, allowing you to make swift adjustments and save both time and money.

THE FIRST STEPS

Okay, so you're convinced that you need to market your health care practice online. Where do you start? Well, before you run out and set up a website, start posting on Facebook, and ask patients to review you on Healthgrades, there a few things you want to do first.

1. **Establish a point person**–Whether this is you or another member of your staff, someone needs to be in charge of coordinating your practice marketing efforts, to ensure that your marketing plan is implemented consistently across all platforms.

2. **Define your target patients**–Internet marketing all starts with a clear understanding of who you are trying to attract. You can do this by creating Patient Personas, fictitious archetypes for the kind of patients you want–and don't want. We'll discuss this in

more depth in the next chapter.

3. **"Ghost" your competitors**–Once you've defined which patients you want to visit your practice, you need to take a look at what others in your area are already doing. This way, you can understand what patients are experiencing with other practices–and what you can do better.

4. **Define your Strengths, Weaknesses, Opportunities, and Threats (SWOT)**–Now that you're armed with an understanding of your local competitors, you can look inward and define the current Strengths, Weaknesses, Opportunities, and Threats of your practice. This will help you determine what makes you different from other practices, so that you can best position yourself with the patients in your market.

5. **Determine your unique selling proposition (USP)**–From your SWOT analysis you can determine your USP. Your USP is important to develop and articulate–it's the reason a patient would choose you over other providers. Without a USP, it's impossible to position your practice and build messaging for ad campaigns.

6. **Document your brand voice**–With your SWOT and USP determined, you can move on to documenting your brand voice, or how you want to describe your practice. This will determine the tone taken on your website and social media profiles, as well as the selection of topics on your blog.

7. **Conduct keyword research**–At this point, you have almost everything you need to get started. The final data point you'll want before creating a plan and implementing your marketing platform software comes through conducting keyword research. Since search engines are the number one driver of new patient acquisition for most practices, having a clear understanding of what patients are looking for in and around your specialty will

help you focus your efforts properly. This topic will be explained further in Chapter 4.

8. Create a Plan–Of course, before you start marketing, you need a plan. The purpose of the first six steps along the way is to give you the knowledge and insights required to create a plan that can achieve your goals. This plan should also help keep you on track and ensure your continued progress.

9. Implement a practice marketing platform–Last, but certainly not least, you need to implement a marketing platform that will help you automate efforts, ensuring you are as efficient as possible. Your practice marketing platform will give you and your team the tools to execute on your efforts. It will also ensure your campaigns are being tracked, so you can easily make tweaks and determine ROI.

Internet marketing can be a powerful way to grow your practice, but proceed with caution. The internet changes daily – heck, Google had a half-dozen updates just last year. What works today may not work tomorrow, meaning there's a lot to stay up-to-date on. That doesn't mean you shouldn't be using internet marketing to grow your practice; just know that you need experience, expertise, and time in order to be successful.

GETTING STARTED WITH INTERNET MARKETING CHECKLIST:

- ☐ A point person has been established to lead practice marketing efforts.
- ☐ Current online marketing and presence performance benchmarks are established.
- ☐ Target patients have been defined and analyzed.
- ☐ Competitive practices in your market are known and have been analyzed for opportunity.
- ☐ You have determined your practice's USP, as well as analyzed all relevant strengths, weaknesses, opportunities, and threats.
- ☐ A brand voice has been crafted, to shape how you will describe your practice in your online marketing efforts.
- ☐ Keyword research has been used to determine target keywords patients use in searches.
- ☐ Practice marketing goals are documented and understood by staff.
- ☐ A formal internet marketing plan is in place and being used to guide efforts.
- ☐ Practice marketing metrics have been established and are monitored consistently.
- ☐ Internal stakeholders and owners are meeting frequently to discuss marketing progress and to update the plan accordingly.

CHAPTER 2

UNDERSTANDING YOUR TARGET PATIENTS

At the beginning of any successful internet marketing effort is an exploration of the patients you want to bring into your practice. Patient acquisition requires targeted practice marketing, and targeted practice marketing requires a comprehensive understanding of your current patients; not only the patients you want to attract more of, but also the ones you wouldn't mind seeing less of. Without a comprehensive understanding of these patients, your efforts will lack direction, waste time (and money), and may actually hurt practice growth.

Instead of thinking about your patients and potential patients as a nebulous group of thousands of unique individuals, each with dramatically different goals, conditions, and circumstances, a marketing best practice is to develop "Patient Personas." Each Patient Persona is a fictional person that accurately serves as a granular representation of a particular group of patients, who have significant similarities in the way of values, beliefs, and motivations. *Personas should be used to influence nearly every decision about your practice,* including your website content and design, your advertising, and the people with whom you network.

For example, if you were an orthopedic surgeon, two personas you may have are young athletes who have been injured playing a sport and elderly people who have developed pain as a result of their body's natural aging process. Clearly, each of these personas will have dramatically different needs, and will therefore respond to different types of marketing. The older patients are more likely to access the web on a desktop or laptop computer, while the younger athletes are more accustomed to using smartphones and tablets. Research also shows that older populations prefer text content, while younger people more readily consume video content.

Determining your target Patient Personas (who you are trying to attract more of), as well as your Negative Patient Personas (who you are trying to attract less of), is crucial to bringing the right types of patients through your door.

Creating and posting content on your practice website geared toward the average person searching online is a mistake.

You overlook the individual by pursuing the average, by providing content for the many.

Your practice marketing, to be most effective, needs to address one person...your persona. Don't address readers as though they were all seated together in an auditorium. When people read your practice's messaging, they do so as an individual. Write as though you are writing a personal letter to each of them, and see just how powerful the concept of the Patient Persona is!

For example, rather than crafting your practice's messaging for "married women between the ages of 25 and 34 with one or two children and an annual income over $50,000," you should gear your messaging toward a singular persona:

Sarah Smith

- 29 years old
- BA in English
- Married for six years
- 2 children

Sarah works at a call center (part-time) and is raising her two children (a boy of 2 and a 6-month-old girl). She is in charge of setting medical appointments for the family, and brings her children to the doctor for routine visits. One of her children has recurring chest infections and requires frequent medical care. Sarah is a non-smoker, and runs a few times a week to stay in shape for the 5k's in which she regularly participates. Sarah also cares for her aging parents, who need some degree of assistance to ensure that their health needs are met.

Isn't it easier to think of Sarah as a real person, rather than a collection of demographic information? See how much easier it would be to develop messaging that will be of interest to her and that will address her needs?

To develop a useful Patient Persona, you must first gain a comprehensive understanding of your current patient population.

By doing this, you will discover what demographics make up your largest patient percentages, establish geographic insights into where they come from, and learn their unique psychographic data. The best way to gather this information is actually quite simple: conduct an audit on your current patients.

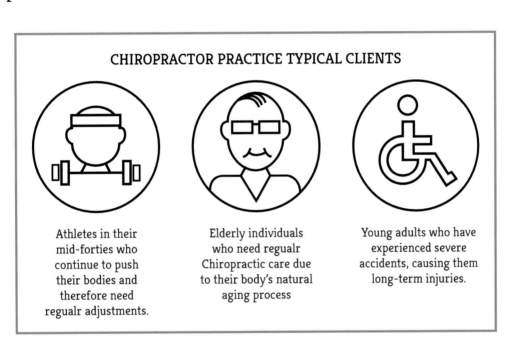

CHIROPRACTOR PRACTICE TYPICAL CLIENTS

Athletes in their mid-forties who continue to push their bodies and therefore need regualr adjustments.

Elderly individuals who need regualr Chiropractic care due to their body's natural aging process

Young adults who have experienced severe accidents, causing them long-term injuries.

The easiest and most scalable way to do this is through a patient survey, which can be sent out via email or completed by patients while in your waiting room. You can even incentivize them with a prize or gift to ensure high completion rates. Other methods to acquire patient information include using your already-existing databases, conducting personal interviews, or even engaging in some educated speculation based on what you already know about certain patients.

Here are some examples of the topics, and specific questions, you should include in your survey:

- **Background Information**–Details about their role in health care ("Do you schedule appointments for your whole family?"), information about their household (number of children, the family's general health, whether or not they have insurance)

- **Demographic Information**–Gender, age, place of residence, income, education level, online resources used to research health questions, online/social platforms used for entertainment purposes

- **Psychographic Information**–Ethnicity, level of tech-savviness, communication preferences, interests and hobbies, other questions specific to your city or town

- **Goals and Challenges**–Primary and secondary health goals, primary and secondary health challenges

- **Constructive Ways to Improve**–"Name three improvements we could implement to make your visits more enjoyable"

A simple survey has a powerful ability to shape what you know (and don't know) about your patients. In turn, this knowledge can help you begin to identify your patients' different needs.

As a byproduct of this exercise, you will also notice undesirable patient silos, referred to as Negative Patient Personas. These are patients that, though you can successfully treat them, are not the most engaging, rewarding, or profitable patients for your practice; in other words, patients on which you would not be interested in spending money to proactively bring into your practice. Correspondingly, your marketing and branding efforts will soon have the capacity to hyper-focus on messaging that will resonate with each desirable silo, and avoid messaging which might attract Negative Patient Personas.

NEGATIVE PATIENT PERSONA

The client archetypes you want to avoid. Less commonly used but play an important role.

So, now that the hard part of gathering all your patient data is complete, what's next?

Start organizing the similarities among your patients into different groups; these will soon become your Patient Personas. The final step is to label your personas with appropriate names, images, and quotes (drawn from your surveys and/or interviews). That's it – you've completed your Patient Personas!

Now comes the fun part. Begin reviewing your competitors' websites, social media profiles, and advertising initiatives.

· Who are they targeting?

- What is their unique selling proposition (USP)?
- How can you differentiate your practice in the minds of your Patient Personas?
- Is there a branding "blind spot" in the market on which your practice can capitalize?

By developing target Patient Personas, tapping into your resources, and conducting competitor research, you will be able to focus your marketing strategies on messaging that will best resonate with the patients you want to attract, thereby delivering the greatest return on investment.

UNDERSTANDING YOUR TARGET PATIENTS CHECKLIST

- ☐ Determine demographic and psychographic information that may be valuable.
- ☐ Gather persona information via surveys, research, and experience.
- ☐ Develop relevant target Patient Personas.
- ☐ Develop Negative Patient Personas, if applicable.
- ☐ Develop enough Patient Personas that the majority of your typical patients are represented.
- ☐ Use personas developed to create practice marketing that will resonate with your personas, and to make practice decisions.
- ☐ Review the respective USPs and target personas of competitor websites, social media profiles, and advertising campaigns.
- ☐ Use gathered information to differentiate your practice.

CHAPTER 3

THE ANATOMY OF AN EFFECTIVE PRACTICE WEBSITE

We're way past simply advising that every medical practice needs a website. Today, the challenge facing health care professionals is putting up a website that actually contributes the bottom line. Most practices are still held back with a basic brochure site that features only scant educational information. This is no longer enough; not if you want your medical practice to be relevant online, let alone successfully bring in patients through the internet.

A survey conducted by the health information network Surescripts found that patients are more likely to select a digitally proficient doctor if given a choice, and far less likely to leave one. Your website is a crucial component in demonstrating your practice's digital sophistication. It should not only reflect your professional success, but should also clearly articulate your mission and present real-life stories about how your work has positively impacted patients. Remember: your website is not a trophy room, nor is it meant for your peers; it's for your patients. With that in mind, since patients are increasingly searching for and comparing physicians online, your website should be a hub for all of your practice marketing efforts.

When it comes to building and maintaining a practice website patients want to visit and use, it helps to first understand what they're looking for. Patients want a modern and informative website, containing:

- Practice location(s) and hours of operation
- Contact information
- Treatment information
- Doctor and staff credentials
- Ability to schedule an appointment
- Patient reviews
- Insurances accepted

If these strike you as basic requests, you're correct; this information can easily be communicated through a simple, yet comprehensive, website. Unfortunately, many practices fail to do even this, displaying incomplete or inaccurate information that does little to help patients. Ensuring you have this basic information listed will enable the beginning of a positive patient experience, and start to set you apart from your competition.

ATTRACTING NEW PATIENTS TO YOUR PRACTICE

Driving organic traffic to your website is crucial to bringing in new patients. That means your website needs a strong search engine optimization (SEO) strategy, one that is geared toward ranking highly in local search results. This is accomplished by targeting the right keywords for your specialty, those that answer the specific questions local patients are asking about the conditions you treat and the treatments you offer at your practice. It also requires putting up content that attracts backlinks, the key driver of high search engine rankings. Both SEO and content marketing will be discussed in greater depth in the following chapters.

When visitors arrive, your website needs to give them an immediate reason to stay and look around instead of bouncing away. Your homepage needs to communicate clearly who and what you treat, so that potential patients know that they're in the right place. It should feature your practice's unique selling proposition as well as your credentials, and should offer patients the ability to schedule an appointment. Photos of your office and your staff should be used heavily throughout the website to get patients accustomed to seeing your practice; you want to be a familiar face before they even step through your doors.

You also need to provide clear, easy navigation to the information patients are most interested in finding: what services and treatments you provide, what insurances you accept, your theory of care, and basic contact information. While you don't want to cram all of this material onto your homepage, you should strive to make it readily apparent where on your site the information can be found.

Lastly, provide patient reviews, stories, and recommendations that act as social proof of your expertise. Patient and colleague testimonials regarding the care you've provided them are valuable, as are any media quotes or references you may have acquired. Social proof is the new word-of-mouth, so make sure all your website visitors see the great things other people say about you.

POSITIONING YOUR PRACTICE AS AN AUTHORITY

Not everyone coming to your website is ready to be a patient. They may be researching a specific medical issue, with which they or a loved one are dealing, or they may just be curious about a more general medical condition. In either case, they're looking for authoritative information.

Your website needs to contain the content that answers their questions. You can do this through blog posts, a "Patient Resources" section, or even downloadable content; in other words, anything that allows you to share important information, current news, and your latest advances with your patients.

Good content to post on your website's blog can include articles like "How to Prepare for Ankle Surgery" or "What Your Doctor Needs to Know That Most Patients Don't Share." You can also use this section to offer ongoing patient education, commentary on medical trends, and even new patient promotions.

Posting this sort of material serves multiple purposes. Firstly, valuable content keeps patients glued to your site and coming back for more information. Secondly, it builds a positive relationship with new patients, establishing your authority and credibility. Finally, it attracts those backlinks we talked about earlier. As more websites link back to your page, Google assigns more authority to your site, and therefore ranks it higher in search results.

Other types of content that build your practice's authority with prospective patients (and Google) include links to press clippings, personable, information-rich physician and staff bios, and individual pages dedicated to each condition you treat and treatment you provide. All of these pages should have titles, headings, content, and descriptions optimized based on keyword research (see Chapter 4 for more information on keyword research).

ESTABLISHING AND STRENGTHENING YOUR RELATIONSHIP WITH PATIENTS

The authority you can establish as an informative, engaging resource is an important part of forming the relationship you want between your practice and prospective patients. While most of the content you create informs these patients, you also need to develop obvious channels that encourage your website visitors to come see you.

You want to insert calls-to-action (CTAs) throughout your site and blog that provide ways for patients to connect with you, whether they want to schedule an appointment, sign up for your newsletter, or simply contact your office with a concern. One CTA that will open an ongoing channel of communication between your practice and your patients is the inclusion of links to your social media profiles on your website, thereby encouraging visitors to follow your practice on Facebook or Instagram. Another call-to-action can involve the promotion of links to specific content within your website, such as staff biographies or particularly popular blog posts.

Building an email list, one that includes current and potential future patients, is another important step in strengthening relationships with patrons of your practice. This is where gated content can play an important role. Gated content refers to high value material that is only made available to people willing to share their email address with you. Gated content can take the form of a newsletter or a special eBook on a particular condition or treatment.

REDUCING ADMINISTRATIVE FRICTION BETWEEN YOUR PRACTICE AND YOUR PATIENTS

Make your website easy to use. Don't make visitors work to find what they need. Start with navigation that's intuitive and obvious. Place click-to-call and online scheduling links on every page so patients who are ready to get in touch with you can do so right away. The practice name, address, and phone number should be located in the footer of every webpage; the practice phone number should be listed in the top right corner as well, so patients can find it easily.

Your site must also be optimized for mobile devices. With the usage

of smartphones and tablets soaring (mobile searches started outpacing desktop searches a couple years ago), it is imperative that your website work just as flawlessly on a smartphone or tablet as it does on a computer. A mobile-optimized practice website carries all the attraction, ease, and authority of your desktop website.

Finally, your website should capture patient demand and demographic information and provide metrics for future campaign optimization via an online analytics program. Remember, if you're anticipating having thousands of patients visit your website every year, you should procure as much data from them as possible. By tracking activity on your practice website, you can use the information gathered to make objective decisions about content and advertising that will grow your practice. These are often overlooked aspects of a practice website, and will be explored in greater depth in Chapter 11.

THE ANATOMY OF AN EFFECTIVE MEDICAL PRACTICE WEBSITE CHECKLIST:

- ☐ The current website design is clean and modern.
- ☐ The website is easy to use and information is easy to find.
- ☐ The practice name, address, and phone number are found on every page, including a phone number in the top right corner.
- ☐ There is the ability to schedule an appointment online.
- ☐ There is a contact page with full practice contact details.
- ☐ There is a page for every condition treated.
- ☐ There is a page for every procedure or treatment you perform.
- ☐ There is a page for each of the main practitioners.
- ☐ Photos of the practice, reception area, examination rooms, equipment used, etc. are found throughout the website.
- ☐ Reviews and other patient and professional testimonials are prominently featured.
- ☐ There is a blog with current articles and information related to your practice, the conditions you treat, and the treatments you offer.
- ☐ New content is posted frequently to support monthly marketing campaigns.
- ☐ There is an easily visible way to subscribe to the practice's email newsletter.
- ☐ Each of the website's pages is optimized based on industry keyword research.
- ☐ The website looks and functions the same, or extremely similarly, on all devices.
- ☐ The website looks and functions the same on all popular web browsers.
- ☐ An online analytics program is set up to track the activity of visitors to your website.

CHAPTER 4

IMPROVING YOUR PRACTICE'S SEARCH VISIBILITY

Believe it or not, 80 percent of internet users – that's 93 million Americans – search online for health information, according to a Pew survey. Instead of pulling out a phone book and flipping through the yellow pages to find a health care provider, your patients are increasingly turning to Google or Bing. What's more, the majority of patients visiting your website aren't doing so because of paid ads, social media, or word-of-mouth referrals. According to a study by the marketing company Conductor, 64 percent of your potential website traffic comes from organic search results – meaning a patient typed a search term into Google, your website appeared, and they clicked on through.

With searches for online health information now the third most popular online search activity, you want to be sure your practice is listed, or "ranking," prominently in the relevant searches that your patients are making every day. This task is imperative to growing your practice's visibility online, and it should be at the top of your internet marketing priorities.

The first step to improving your search rankings lies in understanding what your target patients are searching for, as it relates to the conditions, treatments, and procedures related to your practice. This can be done by simply jotting down the terms patients use when describing their symptoms and ailments. You can then enhance and refine those descriptions by performing keyword research.

WHAT IS KEYWORD RESEARCH?

Keyword research is the practice of using online tools to determine which search phrases potential patients are entering into a search engine to find the conditions you address and the treatments you provide.

Keyword research is the lynchpin of any successful search engine optimization (SEO) strategy, since it puts you in the position of knowing patient intent. Keyword research helps to identify, evaluate, and select the relevant words and phrases for which your website pages should be optimized. All of this makes the job of positioning, marketing, and optimizing your practice online easier than ever before.

TYPES OF KEYWORDS

A keyword or keyword phrase (a series of words) is a query term entered into a search engine or website by a patient, and can be classified by length as well as intent. Broad keywords are those of two or fewer words, while long tail keywords are more specific searches of three or more words (in the context of medical searches, a broad keyword may be something like "chiropractor" while a long tail keyword would be "chiropractor in Chicago"). Brand keywords refer to search queries that specifically target an individual practice or practitioner.

Some keywords are classified as "find" keywords, which indicate the searcher is attempting to locate a medical provider, others are labelled "evaluate" keywords, to signify that the searcher is attempting to learn more about a specific medical practice, and a third group is comprised of "decide" keywords, which show that a searcher is now looking to make contact with an individual provider.

There also exists a difference of intent between singular and plural keywords. Patients who use plurals are often looking for more than one option and want to learn about more than one provider. Patients who use singulars are often looking for a more immediate choice and may be likely to make a quick decision on a provider.

The reporting of keywords and their usage data is not an exact science, since most search engines and websites do not make actual query data available. This means that keywords found through research are often different from the actual search queries of patients, which can result in discrepancies in traffic received via various keywords. The reason for this is simple – everyone thinks and acts upon their needs, wants, and interests in a different manner, using slight variations in phrasing or perhaps even misspelling a word. Google reinforces this fact, reporting that up to 80 percent of the total daily search queries entered into their search interface have never been entered before. This is a primary reason why Google heavily pushes the suggested searches that drop down as you begin to enter a query.

In order to get the most out of keyword research, it's important to understand that traffic estimates are relative and vary. Use them as a guide, but never an absolute!

KEYWORD RESEARCH TOOLS

When it comes to finding and evaluating which keywords to use in your various campaigns, there are a number of tools that you can use.

Wordtracker
Wordtracker is a paid keyword research tool that gives you access to licensed search engine query data. The data allows you to generate lists and view the competitiveness of a particular keyword, as well as tap some of Google's AdWords data.

Google Keyword Planner
For health and medical practices with a Google AdWords account, Google offers access to the Google Keyword Planner. This tool generates lists of suggested keywords and provides data on how frequently patients use them in searches.

Google AdWords Keyword Estimator
This free tool will give you estimated search and per-click cost data. This tool is excellent for estimating how much traffic your AdWords campaigns can generate and approximately how much it will cost to advertise for certain patient searches.

Keyword ideas		Competition
+ Add keywords Download ▾ Estimate search traffic		
☐ **Keyword**		**Competition**
☐ advertising on the internet	🔍	
☐ what is network marketing	🔍	
☐ google adwords training	🔍	
☐ pay per click	🔍	
☐ web developers	🔍	

Google Insights for Search

The Google Insights tool is an excellent way to gather data on a particular search term, providing information on interest trends, regional interest, and related searches. This tool is perfect for comparing similar keywords in order to decide on which to concentrate.

Google Trends Keyword Demand Prediction

Google Trends is a nifty tool to help spot keywords related to a specific topic or genre. It gives you historical data about the performance of keywords and websites, as well as alternative searches and websites.

Microsoft AdCenter Keyword Forecasting

Similar to the Google AdWords Keyword Estimator, the Microsoft Keyword Forecasting tool gives you information about how many times a particular term has been searched for.

KEYWORD RESEARCH CAMPAIGN IN 5 EASY STEPS

1. Pull a List

The first step in a keyword research campaign is to pull a full list of keywords for the topic that you are researching. The most useful tools to help you with this are Wordtracker or Google's Keyword Planner. You can also use the Google Trends tool to find some alternatives if the list you pull is too small, or if you want an additional data set.

2. Relevancy

With a full list of keywords in front of you, remove keywords that are irrelevant. Ask yourself, "Is this keyword relevant to what I'm offering patients?" One bit of advice at this step is to consider putting some of the keywords into Google or another search engine to see what results are generated – you might be surprised by what you find.

3. Organize

Now that you've got a more concentrated list, it is time to organize it by sub-topic. This will give you much smaller groups of keywords to work with and also reveal how the general patient populace searches for a specialty or treatment (allowing you to make presumptions for further campaigns in the future).

4. Competitiveness

At this point, your list should be tight and organized. From here, you want to identify the competitive nature of each keyword. To do this, use the competitive ranking data for the keywords provided by both Google and Wordtracker.

5. Cost and ROI

The last step in the keyword research process is to estimate the cost of the keyword if you were to have a paid advertisement displayed when a patient entered that word in a search query (discussed further in Chapter 10), and the potential return on investment (ROI) of doing so. The best tool for calculating keyword costs is the Google AdWords Keyword Estimator.

SEARCH ENGINE OPTIMIZATION

Once keyword research is completed and you know what your potential patients are searching for, you're ready to move on to the other aspects of SEO.

SEO encompasses best practices and tactics that ensure your website is one of the first non-paid listings in the search engine results for health conditions and medical treatments related to your specialty. There is no one-size-fits-all approach to SEO, as each search engine has its own complex algorithm and ranking system; Google, for example, has over 400 ranking factors that are taken into account before search results are displayed. These algorithms are not only complex, but often updated. In fact, Google released six updates in 2016 alone, a trend that is likely to continue into the future. Therefore, if your website doesn't keep up with the times and continue to comply with the best practices of the day, you could find yourself missing out on patients.

So how do search engines work?

Originally conceived and modeled after a traditional card catalog, search engines came about in response to the need to provide order to the thousands and eventually millions of websites on the internet. Search engines use what can be thought of as "exact match" thinking – they want to find search query results that are the closest match and the most relevant to a particular user's search.

To quickly search the billions of pages on the web, search engines use "web crawlers," or "spiders," to capture the content of a website and store it in their indices. When a potential patient searches for your specialty or a related condition, the search engine queries its database of websites, using its algorithm to display the relevant web pages for the search. Pages that score the highest according to the algorithm appear at the top of the search page, while less relevant pages appear at the bottom or on subsequent pages.

ELEMENTS OF SEO

A properly optimized website requires focused efforts on three different elements: off-site SEO, on-site SEO, and technical SEO.

OFF-SITE SEO

Off-site SEO involves improving the search engine ranking factors that are not directly associated with your website.

To determine and validate that a website is reputable, search engines look at a number of data points. For a health care website, these factors include links to the site from other web pages, listings of the practice in online directories, and reviews on profiles like Google My Business. To a search engine, if you have a lot of links to your practice website from other, popular sites, accurate practice directory listings, and a high volume of reviews, your practice will be identified and distinguished as a place that a patient would want to find and make use of. This makes *third-party links, listings (or citations), and reviews the three most important factors for good off-site SEO.*

Engaging in marketing activities such as blogging and social media has a positive effect on your SEO, as these efforts not only result in ensuring that you have pages on your website dedicated to each of the relevant keyword searches you are targeting, but those pages provide additional opportunities for other websites to link back to your own. Search engines like Google see these backlinks as an indicator of quality—if a well-known site with a good reputation links to information on your site, Google sees it as a sign that your information is valuable, and it improves your search engine rankings for searches related to that page accordingly.

Backlinks are only as good as the site they're on, however. A backlink on a spammy or low-value site will actually hurt your SEO; search engines will lower your rankings or even blacklist your site if you have too many suspicious backlinks.

The best backlinks happen organically, when you produce valuable content that makes reputable websites or organizations want to link back to you. Lending out your expertise, whether through written content for another website or an interview on a popular podcast, can be a great way to develop backlinks and reach a wider audience.

Sponsoring local events (charity fundraisers, non-profit organizations) or volunteering basic services to schools or other area institutions can also result in a much higher public profile for your practice, as well as the opportunity to receive further backlinks from the websites of the organizations you would be helping. Don't forget to request clubs, community, and professional associations that you either donate to or of which you are a member to list your practice website on their own.

Get your name out there alongside the kind of information and services your patients are looking for and you'll get plenty of organic backlinks to help you gather more patients from searches.

Claiming and updating all of your online professional profiles – beyond just Healthgrades and Yelp – with accurate, consistent, and up-to-date information will provide you with additional links that will help your website rankings improve. The more times your practice's name, address, phone number, and website are linked to from claimed listings, the higher your practice will appear in search engine results for related keyword searches.

In addition, consistently soliciting reviews from patients will signal to Google and other search engines that you're popular with patients and should appear highly for localized searches, especially for the growing number of patients on mobile phones.

ON-SITE SEO

On-site SEO focuses on improving aspects of your website, mainly optimizing the contents of individual pages for the keywords that are being targeted.

On-site SEO efforts start with keyword research, which determines what search phrases patients in your area are using to find practices like yours. If you don't have pages targeting the search phrases patients are entering into Google, it's highly likely that you will not appear.

In general, your practice website should have a homepage that targets your core search phrase (i.e. "Dermatologist in Buffalo"), a biographical page that targets the provider's name (i.e. "Dr. Aaron A. Awesome"), and a page for every condition treated and every treatment offered. Those pages should be written for the patient, but also use the search phrase throughout. That way, search engines will understand that the page is about the search phrase topic.

Search engines like Google also love authoritative content that explores topics in depth, so don't be stingy with showing you're a leader in your field. While you don't want to bore your patients, you do want them to be fairly well educated, so try to make each page on your website 750 – 1,000 words in length. A great way to build an authoritative page that patients will love is to answer the questions they commonly ask about a particular topic while they are in your office.

Another key to good on-site SEO is to consistently post fresh content. This can be accomplished by updating existing pages with new material (such as videos, infographics, and images), or by adding new educational blog posts that speak to news, trends, and other regionally (or even seasonally) relevant items.

Finally, as Google and other search engines focus on showing patients search results that include practice websites located close to them, including your name, address and phone number on every page ensures search engines know your local focus.

TECHNICAL SEO

Technical SEO includes all of the "hidden" search engine ranking elements, and usually requires knowledge of website development to achieve adherence to best practices and correction of any issues that may arise. Technical SEO efforts ensure your website is fast-loading, coded using best practices, and is easy for search engine spiders to scan and include in their search indices.

As devices, internet speeds, and patients get faster, search engines need your website to keep up. Patients' attentions spans are shorter than ever and they have no time to wait for a slow-loading website. If you haven't updated or rebuilt your website in the past couple of years, your competitors who have are likely getting a boost in their rankings from Google.

Using tools like Google Search Console and Bing Webmaster Central can help you diagnose technical errors and create a site index, so you can ensure your website has the best chance of being seen. When you claim your website on Google or Bing, you can submit a sitemap and a robots file so the search engines can easily crawl and search your site. They also check for technical problems, like page errors, and provide instructions on how to fix them. These are just two of a number of tools that you can use to see how fast your website loads and what can be done to make it work faster.

You can always just do it yourself, as well. Put yourself in your patient's shoes – pull out your mobile, Google your specialty (or your practice), and see if you like what you see.

Did you show up in the search results? How long did it take for your website to load? Is your website mobile-friendly? If you're not sure, or not happy with what you find, you probably have a technical SEO issue that needs correcting.

SEO RANKING FACTORS

Search engine optimization is a continually changing field, and what works today may not work tomorrow. Each search engine has many factors that affect search rankings, each is weighted differently, and those weights can change over time. To date, however, links and content are the most important SEO ranking factors.

1. Links

Without links, the internet wouldn't be what it is today. Neither you nor your patients would be able to find anything without them. In fact, links are so important that at the core of Google's original thesis and search ranking algorithm is the idea that a website or page with lots of links pointing to it from other websites is likely to be an authoritative source of information.

While the weighting of different ranking factors in Google's and other search engines' algorithms is constantly changing, links will always play the most important role in a successful practice SEO campaign.

With this information in mind, there are a couple of things you can do to optimize your search ranking:

- Increase the total number of unique domains linking to your website. As a way of verifying your website's credibility and authority within your specialty, search engines like to see a large number of unique domains linking to your website from other websites that they already deem authoritative and trustworthy. The more specific the website is to your specialty, and the more trustworthy and popular it is (say, The Wall Street Journal vs. a personal blog), the more valuable the link. As you acquire more high-quality links, your search engine ranking will improve.

- Increase the total number of links to your website. In addition to the number of unique domains linking to your website, you also want a high quantity of backlinks to your website; while Google prizes quality, their search engine algorithms also value quantity. If you're in a small town or just getting started with your SEO efforts, focus on creating good content, spreading that content, and asking patients, friends, and colleagues to share and link to it. Depending on your market and specialty, the number of links you will need in order to be competitive will vary. Increasing your link volume comes with time and consistent efforts!

Note that links and "link building" are two of the most hotly contested areas of SEO. Since links are the foundation of the internet and of search engine rankings, many SEO specialists have taken to launching aggressive campaigns and other schemes to artificially increase the authority (and ranking) of their websites. As a result, Google and other search engines have cracked down on websites with backlink profiles that seem too good to be true, as well as those that have many links which are determined to be of low quality.

In order to prevent any possible negative consequences from soliciting links, aim to make your backlink profile look as if you never intended to build links at all (see chart below for more details).

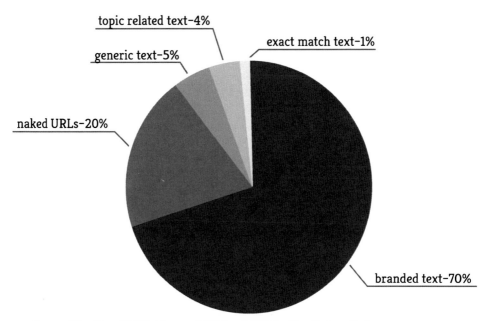

Source: http://LocalSEOGuide.com 2016 Local SEO Ranking Factors Study

2. Keyword usage and on-page content

In the early days of SEO, experts advised keyword stuffing a page –literally using the search phrase over and over again on the page would be enough to rank highly. Back then, search algorithms weren't as advanced as they are today, so as long as your content had plenty of keywords, quality didn't matter.

Today, algorithms have gotten smarter, and while they still look to the page title to determine what the page is all about, they now rate you for the quality of your content. This means search engines are tracking things such as page length, external links (links to other sites), how long a patient stays on the page, and whether a patient goes to other pages on the site or leaves after just one view.

There are a few things you can do to ensure that the content on your website is making the most effective use of keywords:

- **Ensure your page titles are optimized.** Using the data found from your keyword research efforts, make sure each of the page titles on your website is targeting a keyword search phrase that you want to rank highly for. Of course, the page title must also match the context and intent of the patients' search, as well as the content of the page itself. This may require you to create new pages, or rename existing pages.

- **Create accurate, concise content that answers patients' questions.** Using keyword research to optimize a relevant page ensures Google can match the content to a search query, but to be truly successful you must make sure your content is well-written and engaging for the patients who will be reading it. The best way to produce high quality content is to write for your audience, not a search engine. Strive to answer questions related to the search phrase you're targeting in terms your patient can understand. This is not a time to write for peers, but for patients looking for health information online.

- **Implement proper technical structural elements.** Search engine spiders are not as advanced as one might assume. In order to make sense of the content placed on a page, search engines take a number of clues from the technical markup of the page, not just the content itself. To take advantage of this, utilize header tags (H1 and H2, primarily) within your content to structure it into natural sections. You can also discuss implementing local schema mark-up with your webmaster, in order to ensure search engines know your practice's location.

3. Mobile experience and index

The use of smartphones and mobile devices continues to grow exponentially, with no signs of a slow-down in sight. As a result of this technology, Google has proactively taken steps to reward websites that provide searchers with a great mobile experience. Starting in 2016, Google began indexing the mobile versions of websites before indexing the desktop versions, making mobile optimization a huge opportunity (or hurdle) for practice websites. That's right, mobile technology has become so important that you can actually see your search ranking suffer if the mobile version of your website is not properly built and functioning!

Here's how to optimize your website for mobile usage:

- Ensure your website is mobile friendly. Today it's not enough to just have a website – it must be optimized for mobile devices, too. A good way to start this process is to pull out your mobile phone, pull up your website, and try to use it. How fast did it load? Does it look good on a mobile device? Are you able to easily find specific information, contact the practice and/or schedule an appointment?

- Improve your website and page load speeds. Patients using their mobile phones have little tolerance for a slow-loading website. Since Google and others strive to show patients the best search results, they want to show those websites which load quickly. If your website is not up to speed, talk with your webmaster or another professional about ways you can improve its performance.

- Claim your mobile version on Google Search Console. Since the mobile version of your website may very well be different than the desktop version, you will want to claim the mobile version with Google Search Console. This will alert Google to the fact that you have a mobile website, and also show you any technical issues or opportunities for improvement.

- Implement HTTPS. Given the rise in the number of malicious websites, and the coinciding rise in the number of websites that have fallen victim to hacking or other cyberattacks, search engines have increasingly preferred displaying websites that are properly secured. While this is not specific to the mobile version of your website (i.e. this suggestion applies to your desktop version, as well), implementing an SSL certificate is a an easy way to both protect your website and make it more attractive to search engines.

For more specific information on the weighting and value of certain search engine ranking factors, see the chart on the next page.

LOCAL PACK/ FINDER RANKING FACTORS

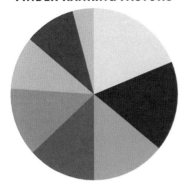

LOCALIZED ORGANIC RANKING FACTORS

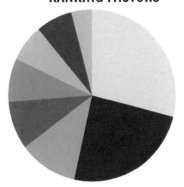

1. My Business Signals–19%
(Proximity, categories, keyword in business title, etc.)

2. Link Signals–17%
(InBound anchor text, linking domain authority, linking domain quantity, etc.)

3. On-Page Signals–14%
(Presence of NAP, keywords in titles, domain authority, etc.)

4. Citation Signals–13%
(IYP/aggregator NAP consistency, citation colume, etc.)

5. Review Signals–13%
(Review quantity, review velocity, review diversity, etc.)

6. Behavioral Signals–10%
(Click-through rate, mobile clicks to callm check-ins, etc.)

7. Personalization–10%

8. Social Signals–4%
(Google engagement, Twitter engagement, etc.)

1. Link Signals–29%
(InBound anchor text, linking domain authority, linking domain quantity, etc.)

2. On-Page Signals–24%
(Presence of NAP, keywords in titles, domain authority, etc.)

3. Behavorial Signals–11%
(Click-through rate, mobile clicks to callm check-ins, etc.)

4. Personalization–9%

5. Citation Signals–8%
(IYP/aggregator NAP consistency, citation colume, etc.)

6. My Business Signals–7%
(Proximity, categories, keyword in business title, etc.)

7. Review Signals–7%
(Review quantity, review velocity, review diversity, etc.)

8. Social Signals–4%
(Google engagement, Twitter engagement, etc.)

Source: http://LocalSEOGuide.com 2016 Local SEO Ranking Factors Study

GOOGLE MY BUSINESS

Google My Business is a free tool offered by Google to help businesses manage their presence on Google-owned properties such as Google Search, Google Maps, and the Google+ social network. Originally, businesses created a page on Google+ for users to find. Google then streamlined business listings by launching Google My Business in 2014, to provide businesses with a one-stop shop to input all of their business information.

Over the last few years, Google has placed increasing emphasis on local search results, as over 85 percent of Google's daily search traffic comes from local searches. *For patients looking for information about health related conditions, injuries, and treatments, Google gives preference to health care providers located closest to the searcher's physical location.*

In order to determine a medical provider's proximity to a patient searching for health care information, Google relies on the data contained in the verified Google My Business profile for the practice and/or provider. This means that if a patient types "Phoenix dentist" into Google, and you have a Google My Business account for your Phoenix-based dental office, your practice has an opportunity to appear as a top listing. If you do not have a verified Google My Business profile, chances are you will not appear.

50

Having a GMB profile also allows your practice to appear in Google's "3-pack." When a user searches for a type of medical practice, Google displays the top three Google My Business profiles near the user in the form of a map, showing the clinic or office location and then a list of the three providers' basic information (name, address, phone number, website, directions, etc.). Unlike organic search results, which take into account ranking factors for your website, appearing in one of the top three slots requires a relevant, up-to-date Google My Business profile.

SETTING UP YOUR GOOGLE MY BUSINESS PROFILE

Setting up your Google My Business page is fairly simple. On the Google My Business homepage, click the "Start Now" button. You'll be redirected to a map where you'll type in either your business name or address.

Once you hit "Search," you'll see a list of potential matches. If your business isn't on the list, just click on the link at the bottom of the search results to add your business.

When creating your business, be sure to fill out each of the following pieces thoroughly.

1. Add a Consistent NAP
It's important to have a consistent name, address, and phone number on your Google My Business page, as well as on your website and elsewhere on the internet. *Google sees each citation of your NAP around the web, and if there are inconsistencies among them, your search ranking will be lowered.* Be sure to use a physical address – Google doesn't allow P.O. boxes to be listed as addresses. Phone numbers should also be local, when possible.

2. Add a Consistent URL
The URL you list should be your website, not a social media page or a landing page. Consistency is also important here – if you have multiple URLs in your mentions around the web, Google views you as

untrustworthy. Using a consistent URL is just as important as using a consistent NAP.

3. Claim Your Business
Once you've entered your business information, Google sends you a postcard at the address you've listed with a verification code. After you receive the postcard, enter the given code to your Google My Business account to complete the process.

4. Add Photos
To personalize your profile page, add an avatar and background image. Your avatar could be a professional headshot, your practice's logo, or a related image. Your background image could be a photo of your building or a related stock image.

5. Choose Your Categories
Google allows you to choose categories into which your business fits. You can pick up to five, but make sure they are relevant. Choose a mix of broad and specific listings, if possible.

Be careful to avoid choosing plurals of categories you already have listed. For instance, if you choose the category "orthopedic surgeon," you don't want to choose "orthopedic surgeons" as well. It's also important to avoid listing services instead of business type as categories. If you listed "shoulder surgery," for example, instead of "shoulder surgeon," Google would penalize your page.

6. Add Your Hours
Potential patients will find it helpful if you post updated hours on your Google My Business page; that way they'll know what times they can call or visit, instead of getting sent to voicemail.

7. Write a Concise "About You" Section
Include a few sentences about you and your practice on your page. Avoid keyword stuffing, but do choose one or two good keywords to throw in so Google and your patients can easily understand what you do.

What If I Have Multiple Locations?

If you practice at more than one office location, you should have a Google My Business page for each location. The practice name at each should be the same, and you should choose the same categories for each.

OPTIMIZING YOUR GOOGLE MY BUSINESS PROFILE

Making it into the local 3-pack on Google – and sometimes just getting a Google My Business listing – can be difficult. Google is picky and has strict guidelines that users must follow; if you don't, we can guarantee that you won't make it into the top three Google search results, and Google may not even approve your GMB profile in the first place.

To sum it up, here are the three C's to keep in mind when optimizing your Google My Business page:

Completeness
Complete every part of your profile. Avoid leaving any blanks when you fill out your information. That means you need to list your website, phone number, accurate business hours, and business categories. Be sure to add multiple photos and videos of your practice and yourself, as well as any photos of your awards and recognitions.

Correctness
It may seem obvious, but if your profile contains inaccurate information, like a wrong phone number, incorrect business categories, or a wrong URL, your page will not show up in the local pack on search results. It's especially important to have a correct address because Google sends a verification card to your physical location. If you don't receive that card, you can't complete your listing.

Consistency
We mentioned it above, but consistency is key. Google searches your web page and all mentions of your practice on the web. If the search results in what Google views as inaccuracies – mismatched URLs, multiple phone numbers, or different practice names – your practice won't be placed in the local 3-pack.

Optimizing a website takes time and patience. New traffic won't necessarily flow in overnight, even if you make the right changes now, but following the practices outlined in this chapter will certainly help improve your website's search visibility.

IMPROVING YOUR PRACTICE'S SEARCH VISIBILITY CHECKLIST:

- ☐ Conduct keyword research to understand what your target patients are searching for in relation to conditions, treatments, and specialties.
- ☐ Create a list of targeted keyword phrases for your practice.
- ☐ Manually check or use marketing software to see where your practice ranks in search results for each keyword phrase.
- ☐ Monitor keyword rankings for each keyword phrase.
- ☐ Match targeted keywords to your appropriate practice web pages.
- ☐ Create pages for every condition you treat and every treatment you offer.
- ☐ Optimize each page title with the desired keyword, based on your keyword research.
- ☐ Localize your website by including your name, address, and phone number on every page.
- ☐ Create and share new content on a regular basis.
- ☐ Solicit credible backlinks to your site.
- ☐ Claim your website on Google Webmaster Central.
- ☐ Claim and optimize your Google My Business profile.

CHAPTER 5

CLAIMING AND MAINTAINING YOUR PRACTICE LISTINGS ONLINE

In a perfect world, patients would begin searching for a practitioner online and immediately find your website, schedule an appointment, and never leave your care. However, that's not how online patient behavior works. A patient's first interaction with your practice will typically be on another website, most likely a business or medical directory like Healthgrades, Superpages, or Yelp. As a result, it should be clear that a major part of any online marketing effort is ensuring your practice has clean data and accurate listings on third-party websites.

Your practice listings, also referred to as citations, contain information such as your name, address, and phone number (NAP), hours of operation, specialties, credentials, photos, and more. It is essential that you find and "claim" all of your online practice listings. Otherwise, you could be missing out on large numbers of patients.

WHAT IS LISTINGS MANAGEMENT?

In the vast world of the internet, hundreds of business and medical directories have sprung up over the years with the goal of helping caregivers and patients find the right provider. You may have gotten a random email or phone call about one, or maybe you've even found one yourself as you explored online.

These directories, many of which are very familiar, often create profiles for you and your practice locations without you even knowing it. In their pursuit of helping patients (and themselves), these directories often buy or scrape data from other sources in order to create your profiles. Sneaky, huh? What's more, this often results in profiles with inaccurate, missing, and/or outdated information, which can have a big impact on your practice.

For one thing, many of these directories are popular with patients searching for a health care provider online. If you have an outdated or inaccurate profile, you risk turning off a potential new patient. After all, you don't want a patient to call a disconnected phone number or show up at a closed location, do you? *Medical practices lose a huge amount of potential patients every year due to inaccurate online listings.*

Secondly, search engines like Google and Bing have historically relied on directories to verify the address of a practice for their Maps products. As a result, search engines have given a boost to practices that have clean NAP information across all of the major directories' profiles, because they are confident in the information's accuracy. The cleaner, more accurate, and more consistent your citations are, the more favorably Google and other search engines will view your practice.

Before going any further, let's talk about these directory listings, or citations.

WHAT IS A CITATION?

A citation is any reference on the internet to your name, address, and phone number (NAP).

Citations can be found complete or partial, with only one or two of the items listed. Some citations are unstructured, while others are structured as part of a webpage's standard information. For instance, a local blogger could list the top five orthopedic surgeons in your city and include your name, address, and phone number – that's an unstructured citation. By contrast, if your NAP is referenced in a directory published by a newspaper or professional website, that would be a structured citation.

While you can't control a citation in a blog or in the newspaper, numerous websites and internet directories allow you to claim your practice's profile and keep this information up-to-date. It's also worth noting that claiming a profile is usually free. In order to take advantage of your listings and citations, you should claim and optimize your profiles so that each citation includes the same NAP information.

WHY ARE CITATIONS AND LISTINGS MANAGEMENT IMPORTANT?

A full 90 percent of local search engine marketing experts say online citations are vital for your local search marketing success, according to a survey by the marketing company BrightLocal. *Citations are one way search engines verify that your medical practice is legitimate.*

After all, anyone can create a website for just about anything these days; if Google or Bing can't find online citations to back up the website's legitimacy, however, they may be hesitant to list it highly in their search results. The growing usage of mobile devices to conduct online searches has also resulted in search engines showing more geographically-influenced results, making the exact location of a clinic or office extremely important.

For instance, if a person searched for "orthopedic surgeon," the first Google results would be the local 3-pack, a listing of the top three local providers. The information displayed is powered by Google My Business profiles, as well as a practice's online citations. In order for Google to confidently display a practice in the local 3-pack, it must first verify that the address and contact information of the practice is consistent and reliable across several sources.

Inaccurate or inconsistent citations make it difficult for search engines to confidently place your practice on the map. It may also signal to them that your practice isn't legitimate or that your information is old and therefore likely to be inaccurate. Accuracy and consistency across all your listings verify that your business really exists and that you're more likely to provide a quality experience to patrons (after all, if you spent the time to claim and update your citations, you're probably doing well by your patients).

Additionally, these profiles increase your visibility online and push traffic to your website. For example, a potential patient may search for "shoulder surgeon" on Google. Since the search is so generic, your website may not appear at the top of search listings; another website like Healthgrades, Vitals, or Yelp may, however. From there, potential patients could find your profile and then click through to your website.

Another important aspect of online citations is that many profile sites allow patients to add a public rating or review. Patient reviews relate first-hand the patient's take on your expertise and skills, and help other patients decide whether or not to choose you for their medical provider. This makes it important that you not only claim, but also monitor many of the profiles on the internet for your business.

Fortunately for you, claiming your practice listings online is not terribly difficult. It is usually done by registering with the respective online directory or review website, which often requires automated phone or text message verification. This can be a time-consuming process, however, so don't plan on getting it all done in one sitting.

MAJOR ONLINE DIRECTORY LISTINGS TO MANAGE

The internet is full of sites where medical professionals can claim their profile and list relevant information. Not all online directories and profile sites are created equal, however. Many of them are a complete waste of time, and others could actually hurt your search engine rankings, as the directory is considered to be spammy by search engines.

Given that it could take you over forty hours to claim all of the major directory listings for you and your practice, it's best to start with the listings that will provide the most impact to your practice's marketing efforts.

MEDICAL AND HEALTH CARE PROVIDER PROFILE WEBSITES

Sites like Healthgrades, RateMDs, Vitals, or WebMD are dedicated specifically to the medical and health care profession. More often than not, these websites are designed to allow patients to find and evaluate providers. Patients can leave reviews to help other patients make decisions about their health care providers, and in many cases can book an appointment with the provider right on their profile page.

GENERAL BUSINESS PROFILE WEBSITES

In addition to the health care and medical specific websites, there are many other websites where all business can be found by those looking for a vendor. Some of these websites (i.e. Facebook) are social media platforms, many of which allow patients to leave reviews. Other websites are more like the yellow pages, a pure directory that only lists your NAP and other business-related information.

These websites include:

- Angie's List–A members-only service provider rating and review website. While more tailored toward home service providers, Angie's List does have a section for medical practices and health care providers.

- Facebook–The leading social networking platform used by millions. Patients are increasingly using this platform to find recommendations for physicians and other health care providers.

- Google My Business–Google's directory of local businesses, which powers Google Maps and local search results.

- **Yelp**–The leading rating and review website for businesses. Yelp often ranks highly for patient health searches, making it one of the more visible websites for patients looking for care online.

- **DexKnows**–An online aggregator of businesses and information that powers dozens of niche and specialty directories. Depending on your specialty, your practice may want to be present on one of their properties.

- **Indeed**–A job posting aggregation website, Indeed is important because businesses that are hiring project a degree of success. Having a profile with a link back to your site can positively influence your search ranking.

- **Superpages**–The online version of the old Superpages phone book, still used by certain demographics. Superpages, like Yelp, ranks highly for many localized health and medical searches.

- **Yellow Pages**–The online version of the Yellow Pages phone book. Yellow Pages is similar to Superpages, although in recent years it has become less visible online as an entry point for patients to find providers.

- **Insider Pages**–A general business directory, similar to Superpages and Yellow Pages in almost every way.

- **Yahoo Loca**–Yahoo's directory of local businesses. These directory listings are used to power Yahoo Local search results, which are prominently displayed in searches for health conditions and health care providers.

Claiming your listings gives you a direct, verified relationship with the online directory and signals that you are a real, legitimate practice. It also establishes your practice as the owner of the listing, giving you control over the content and updates.

When claiming your practice listings, you should include as much information about your practice as allowed. This includes your NAP, information on the conditions you treat and the treatments you offer, your credentials, hours of operation, and, if possible, the types of insurance accepted by your practice. Having this layer of accurate, consistent, and up-to-date practice data across hundreds of online directories will drive both your search engine rankings and website traffic in a powerful way.

In order to maximize exposure for your practice, you should always be creating new practice listings on relevant online directories. Distributing your information to the leading search engines, directories, internet yellow pages (IYPs), and social media networks ensures your business can be found anywhere potential patients are looking for a practice.

If your citations across the internet aren't current, your patients and potential patients are going to have trouble finding your website. If you haven't already done so, take a few minutes to check out your existing profile on some of the sites listed above. Is it accurate? If not, you've got work to do!

CLAIMING AND MAINTAINING YOUR PRACTICE LISTINGS ONLINE CHECKLIST:

- ☐ Manually search for (or use marketing software to find) your practice listings.

- ☐ Catalog each practice listing you find in an Excel spreadsheet or marketing software.

- ☐ Claim each listing for the practice with the respective online directory.

- ☐ Update each directory listing you find with the accurate name, address, and phone number (NAP).

- ☐ Optimize each directory listing with information about practice specialties, treatments, hours, accepted insurances, and photos.

- ☐ Ensure that your directory listings target your keywords and that your practice is properly categorized (for example, if you are a fertility clinic in Cincinnati, make sure you're not listed as a dentist in Columbus).

- ☐ Continuously monitor for new directories and inaccuracies in existing directories, either manually or with marketing software.

CHAPTER 6

ENSURING A POSITIVE ONLINE REPUTATION

On the internet, the influence of user-generated content is growing rapidly. For your medical practice, this means that more and more control of the patient/provider relationship is being claimed by your patients. At no point is the influence of patients more keenly felt than when it comes to online practice reviews and ratings.

Authentic patient reviews and ratings are some of the most compelling marketing content available to practices, as they have the greatest potential to influence new patients, for better or worse. *Online word-of-mouth credibility for your practice is invaluable, and managing your internet reputation is a crucial part of successfully marketing your practice.*

THE IMPORTANCE OF REPUTATION MANAGEMENT

Reputation management involves the solicitation of reviews and ratings from patients after they visit your office, while consistently monitoring your online ratings and reviews on websites like Healthgrades. Many practices today are also monitoring what's being said about them on social media. Reputation management can make patient feedback the heartbeat of your practice and a way to ensure you're providing a high quality patient experience

It used to be that you simply practiced great medicine and patients came through the office doors. In the internet era, *however, your online reputation is your reputation.* Even if a patient is referred to you by another provider or a family member, chances are they're going to check up on you online. If they have been given a few different providers to choose from, what they see about you in online reviews can greatly influence their final decision.

Although less than 10 percent of patients naturally post a rating or review about you or your practice online, unsatisfied patients are the most motivated to complain, according to a survey conducted by the research company Software Advice. This leaves providers who are not proactively soliciting and monitoring reviews with an online presence that doesn't reflect reality. It's your job to ensure that the online incarnation of your practice seen by potential patients matches the offline experience of patients seen by your practice. Even if you're a great doctor, all it takes is a few angry patients to post negative reviews to tarnish your online reputation.

In 2015, 92 percent of consumers read online reviews to determine the reputation of a business or medical practice, according to BrightLocal's Local Patient Review Survey. Forty percent of those consumers made a judgment call after reading only a few reviews. If the top two or three practice reviews a patient sees are negative, they will be less likely to use the provider in question.

Again, imagine that a patient has been given a few names of providers in the area. The patient then begins to research her options, beginning with a simple Google search of "Dr. Smith dentist." The patient is going to see at least four or five different rating or review website profiles for Dr. Smith. If the star ratings on these sites are low across the board, or if the most recent patient reviews are negative on a particular profile, the patient is likely to come away with an unfavorable opinion of the provider. If that same patient then goes to Google with one of the other names she has, "Dr. Jane Doe dentist," and she sees positive reviews across all of her profiles (and there are plenty of them), the patient is likely to have a favorable opinion of the provider

Who do you think she is going to call or make an appointment with online?

Additionally, search engines like Google give favorable weighting in their local search engine results for practices with a large volume of positive reviews. Up to about fifty total reviews, Google will increase the positioning of your listing in their results for searches related to your practice specialty (i.e. "chiropractor," "best dentist in NYC," "dentist Atlanta," etc.). The more reviews your practice has on its Google My Business profile, the more likely you'll be to appear on the first pages of a potential patient's search related to your practice. Medical practices with verified Google listings also see patient ratings and reviews in their Google My Business dashboard, and can reply to them.

Remember, it's in Google's best interest to show the highest-rated providers to patients. With Google driving more new patients to practices than any other online channel, it's crucial to recognize the importance of increasing the number of positive reviews of your practice. While ranking the "best provider" may be subjective, and your opinion of online ratings and review websites low, internet reviews are not going away, and there's high return on investment to an ongoing reputation management campaign.

TOP HEALTH CARE PROVIDER REVIEW AND RATING WEBSITES

As a health care provider, there are several sites you should be aware of when it comes to your professional online reputation.

HEALTHGRADES

Healthgrades is a website that allows patients to search for medical providers or hospitals to receive care. It's also the largest and most widely used doctor review website – in 2013, Healthgrades was the first stop for 43 percent of patients searching for providers, according to the Software Advice survey.

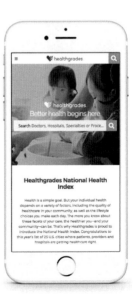

Health care practices can create free profiles on Healthgrades that patients can search when looking for a provider. After their visit, patients can then rate the provider on Healthgrades and leave a review. When a patient searches for a provider, the provider with the best reviews and ratings is often listed at the top of the search.

Since it's the number one site with patients, Healthgrades can't be ignored.

VITALS

Vitals is the second most popular health care provider review website. Additionally, Software Advice found that almost a fifth of patients who use Vitals do so to search for reviews of a specific medical provider. A major difference between Vitals and other popular websites is that Vitals allows patients to compare the cost of one provider or procedure to other similar options.

Vitals calls itself "the most robust and accurate provider database" and claims that it has 90 million members. With such a large number of users, your Vitals profile is important to monitor.

RATEMDS

RateMDs is another health care provider review website, similar to Healthgrades and Vitals. On RateMDs, patients can rate a doctor for knowledge, punctuality, staff, and helpfulness, as well as leave reviews based on their experience.

While not as large as Healthgrades or Vitals, about 24 percent of patients in the Software Advice survey said that RateMDs was their most trusted source of physician reviews. This is enough usage to convince any provider of the need to pay attention to his or her practice's profile on RateMDs.

WEBMD

You've probably already heard of WebMD, the health and medical resource website that gets over 145 million visits per month. WebMD is notorious online, and is often cited by patients as their de facto source for information on their care. What you may not know is that WebMD also has a robust provider directory, which features information about individual physicians.

Given that WebMD is the largest medical and health information website on the internet, it's a no-brainer that you should claim and optimize your profile. The WebMD directory is not just a listing, either – it also features ratings and reviews from patients, making it an important profile and part of your reputation management efforts.

MD.COM

MD.com has a long history among medical review outlets. It was one of the first doctor review websites, and over the past decade has grown into much more. The site now provides tele-health services for both patients and providers through their own mobile app.

MD.com might have changed its focus over the years, but it has never stopped allowing patients to leave reviews of providers on the website. These reviews may have taken a backseat in the context of the site's recent evolution, but with tens of thousands of existing profiles on their website already, you could be one of them without even knowing it. It's therefore in your best interest to check this site out and claim whatever profiles may exist for your practice.

GOOGLE MY BUSINESS

Today, when a patient conducts a Google search for your specialty, the results they see are powered in part by Google My Business. This holds true even if a patient searches directly for your name; in that case, Google displays information from your Google My Business profile on the right-hand side of the results page.

Many marketers focus on Google My Business for its SEO value, but patients can also see reviews left by patients when they search. These include reviews left directly on your Google My Business profile and also aggregated reviews from other websites, such as Facebook and Healthgrades.

Out of all the medical provider review sites, Google My Business reviews may be the most important to manage, as a large majority of patients go to Google first when looking for a provider.

CAREDASH

CareDash is a new venture, a start-up that's taking a fresh approach to patient reviews as it seeks a seat at the table with behemoths like Healthgrades and Vitals. What sets CareDash apart is its focus on furthering transparency in the review process, working to deliver better insights and data to both patients and providers.

With its emphasis on helping the growing number of patients that value user experience and transparency in health care, CareDash is rapidly becoming a go-to starting point for patients in search of a new provider.

FACEBOOK

It's important for health care providers to carefully manage and monitor their Facebook pages because, like Google, Facebook reviews are highly visible – after all, most patients will have their own Facebook profiles. Many patients are also starting to send private messages requesting appointments, something that would be missed by a provider not monitoring his or her profile.

Be careful not to use your personal page as your business page on Facebook. Instead, create a page specifically for your practice so patients aren't seeing your personal posts along with your professional content.

YELP

Last, but certainly not least, there's Yelp.

You know Yelp. You hate Yelp. You love Yelp. You want to Yelp about Yelp.

Yelp, best known for restaurant and retailer reviews, also has a section for health care reviews that is heavily used by patients. Patients leave reviews based on their satisfaction with you as the provider, your staff, and the care they receive. You know, they Yelp. Like Facebook and Google, because Yelp is such a large review website, it's critically important for health care providers to monitor their practices' Yelp profiles.

HOW TO ENSURE A POSITIVE ONLINE REPUTATION

Ensuring you protect your professional reputation requires a plan. Here's one to get you started:

1. Solicit reviews

The best way to prevent negative reviews from damaging your online reputation is to solicit reviews from all your patients. *By having lots of positive reviews coming in on a regular basis, you can minimize the potential damage done by an occasional negative review.*

While unhappy patients are more likely to organically leave a review online, when asked, happy patients are more than willing to leave reviews as well. In fact, a recent survey stated that 90 percent of people left a review when they were asked to do so.

To solicit reviews, there are several different methods you can employ.
- First, ask for a review in-person at your office. This is the best time to ask for a review, because the care your patients just received is still at the top of their minds. You could have patients either fill out a review on their mobile phones or you could place tablets in convenient locations, so patients can post a review as they leave.

• **Second,** you could ask for ratings and reviews via paper forms that patients fill out, either in the office or at home. This works especially well if your patients are older and don't want to post feedback online.

• **Sending follow-up emails** or text messages after the patient visits your office is another great way to solicit reviews. At the end of the email or text message, include a link for the patient to follow to post a review about their care.

Another option, which we at InboundMD recommend to all practices, is to automate the solicitation of reviews using review software such as RepCheckup. These software solutions solicit reviews from patients via email or text message after their visit, ensuring that every patient gets an opportunity to participate, and removing from you the responsibility of having to verbally request feedback from every patient you see.

It is important to note that review sites attempt to manage fake reviews in many ways, including flagging accounts whose reviews are submitted from the same physical location. Consequently, patient reviews should never be faked by people working at your practice(s), as it's inevitable that they will be removed.

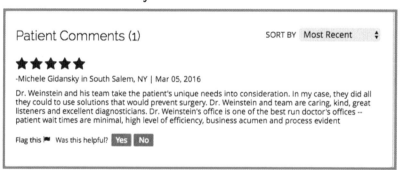

2. Implement a rating and review profile monitoring strategy

It's important to keep track of what your patients are saying about you. Combing the internet to find any mention of your name and reviewing multiple profiles can take hours – hours you don't have. That's where reputation management software such as

RepCheckup comes in handy. RepCheckup monitors your profiles on websites such as Facebook, Google, and Healthgrades in real time, alerting you of new reviews as soon as they are posted.

3. Create approved responses to positive and negative reviews

Monitoring reviews isn't enough to ensure a prolific online reputation. It's also important to recognize patients by responding to both positive and negative reviews. Instead of crafting an individual response to each and every review, create a boilerplate response for positive reviews and another for negative reviews. This makes responding easier, more efficient, and also allows other staff members to post responses for you.

RESPONDING TO NEGATIVE REVIEWS

Negative reviews from patients are going to happen, so don't fret when you see one come in. A few patients will get upset no matter how you treat them or blame all their health and insurance-related issues on you. These are the patients that will leave negative reviews, and it's important to respond to them promptly. The goal is to turn these patients' future experiences into positive ones.

In your response, never get upset and never reveal patient health information. The internet is not the place to get into arguments with patients. Keep your response cool and neutral with no inflammatory language. Also, your responses should not include any specifics about the patient or their condition, in order to comply with the Health Insurance Portability and Accountability Act (HIPAA). Negative reviews with curse words, those that are clearly irrelevant, or those likely to be fake should be flagged as "inappropriate" and left to the website to rescind.

The best advice we can give in the event of a negative review is to take it offline. Instead of continuing the conversation on the review site, respond to the review with something like:

"We strive to provide the best patient care in all situations. We're sorry to hear about your disappointment and want to help. Please contact us at

1-800-999-9999, so we can discuss your situation and what can be done to improve it, immediately. Thanks, Dr. Aaron Awesome."

Once you address the patient's issue on a one-to-one basis, you will likely turn him or her into a happy, long-term patient, as well as show other viewers how you handled the concern. The patient may then withdraw their negative review, make an amendment to it, or even write a second, positive one.

Remember, the best way to fight the potential for negative reviews is to constantly be receiving new positive ones.

OTHER USES FOR ONLINE REVIEWS AND RATINGS

Reviews are an important part of your online reputation, but they're also useful for marketing. A potential patient hearing how great you are from either yourself or your staff is one thing – hearing it from other patients is another.

You can use positive patient reviews on your website, as part of social media graphics, and in videos you post online in order to provide "social proof" of your excellence and build trust with new patients.

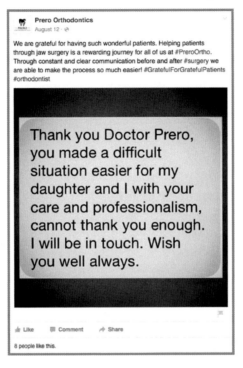

From reflecting the great offline care your practice provides to improving your search visibility and bringing in new patients, having a positive online reputation is an important component to online success. You may not like subjecting yourself to review, but the positives of implementing a reputation management program far outweigh any negatives.

REPUTATION MANAGEMENT: ONLINE REVIEWS AND RATINGS CHECKLIST:

- ☐ Audit each practice's search engine and review site listings.
- ☐ Claim each practice's search engine and review site listings.
- ☐ Update each practice's search engine and review site listings.
- ☐ Solicit reviews from your patients, manually at first and eventually through automated software.
- ☐ Continuously monitor each practice's search engine and review site listings for new reviews.
- ☐ Provide review opportunities or links to review websites on each of your practice websites.
- ☐ Implement an in-practice review cue.

  Respond to positive and negative reviews on behalf of each practice.

CHAPTER 7

BUILDING AUTHORITY WITH CONSISTENT CONTENT

Patients take a number of factors into consideration before choosing a medical or health care provider, including their personal financial situation, health insurance coverage, the geographic location of the provider, and the seriousness of their condition. Additionally, they will seek out differentiators between similar practitioners, such as expertise and experience in the area of care they require. *Building authority through consistent content is an excellent way to go about setting yourself apart from your competition*, and will make choosing your practice an easy decision.

By creating and publishing online content through your website and social media profiles, your practice will become a local (or even national) leader in your specialty. Couple this leadership with a compelling brand voice and you'll be able to better connect with current and potential patients on both professional and personal levels across different content marketing mediums.

WHAT IS CONTENT MARKETING?

In this day and age, your patients are being bombarded by medical information online, and many turn to websites like WebMD or online forums to self-diagnose their ailments. While these resources can be helpful, they often do more harm than good. Your online content – a digital medical library, so to speak – is a much better place for your patients to learn about their health.

The folks at Content Marketing Institute explain the concept well: "Content marketing's purpose is to attract and retain customers by consistently creating and curating relevant and valuable content with the intention of changing or enhancing consumer behavior."

Content marketing involves publishing and sharing online content (blog posts, emails, YouTube videos, or social media posts). Content sets you up as an expert in your field, and it helps you develop a level of trust with potential patients. As they read your content, they are assured that you provide the very best care. Consistently updating your website with fresh content about topics related to your specialty also improves traffic to your website, which will ultimately drive more patients into your office.

One easy way to get content on your site is to create a page for every condition you treat and every treatment you provide. A blog is another good strategy to create specific pages for the keywords and search phrases you want to target in patients' searches.

Blogging is almost old as the internet itself. In fact, I started my first blog in 2005! Initially, bloggers used "weblogs" as personal diaries where they posted updates about their lives or topics that interested them.

Now, due to their personal and relaxed tone, medical professionals use blogs as a way to humanize their practice and engage with patients. Blog content typically consists of written articles, but it can include videos and other visuals, like infographics, as well. When people find you online and read your content, they give you something valuable in return: their time. The more often they read your content, the more likely they will be to visit your practice.

Remember, content marketing differs from direct marketing. Instead of advertising a few times in the paper, on television, or sending post cards in the mail, effective content marketing programs require an ongoing commitment. You have to create a plan for continuously producing content and then stick to that plan for it to ultimately work for you.

WHY CONTENT MARKETING IS IMPORTANT FOR MEDICAL AND HEALTH CARE PRACTICES

Consumers – your patients – have gotten pretty good at tuning out advertising noise. Online, they only see content they consider valuable, ignoring banner advertising and pop-up's almost anywhere they appear. With 80 percent of Americans searching online for medical information, according to Pew survey data, and 20 percent of those searching for a specific doctor, it's more vital than ever that your content marketing be up to par.

Content marketing gives patients what they're looking for: valuable, helpful information that makes them feel comfortable coming into your office. Adding content marketing to your overall marketing strategy establishes you as an expert in your field and helps your patients turn to you for medical information, instead of to more generic websites.

Blogging is the core of content marketing. Keeping an updated blog provides engaging content for your patients and helps sets your brand apart from other health care practices. It's a way for you to keep your patients updated, to educate them on their health and medical needs, and to share important information. It's also the basis for your social media participation – without lots of content to publish on your profiles, it's tough to effectively participate.

THE TYPE OF CONTENT PATIENTS WANT

PATIENT-CENTERED

Your content marketing should be patient-centered. Before you come up with topics or choose the particular medium you'll publish in, consider what your patients want and need. Sports medicine providers, for example, will need different types of content than pediatricians.

Put yourself in your patient's shoes. Use the Patient Personas you've developed to help think through their scenarios, and walk through how they might search for answers to their medical questions.

For instance, if you're writing about carpal tunnel syndrome, take some time to understand some of the ways patients may try to alleviate pain without surgery. How does carpal tunnel affect their day-to-day lives? How do they try to cope? What search terms would they type into Google? What would they ask their friends on Facebook?

Understanding how patients are thinking about their conditions and the treatments you provide will allow you to create content that captures their attention. You can also ask them what topics interest them the most or use the questions they ask most frequently in the office as initial topics to explore.

Another thing to consider as you write for your audience is that most of them won't understand medical jargon. If possible, avoid words that aren't readily understood by the general public. If you must use technical terms, explain their meaning and provide a link to the dictionary definition. To see how easy to read your content is, consider running it through a Flesch-Kincaid test, available online. The closer your score is to 100, the easier it will be to read.

You should aim for a score above 60, to keep your writing on an 8th or 9th grade reading level.

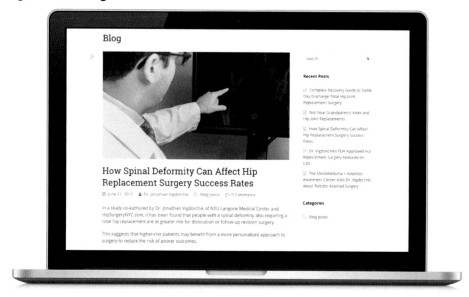

NOT ADVERTISING OR ADVICE

Keep in mind that your content should not sound like advertising. The best content doesn't necessarily talk about the great care patients will receive at your practice. Instead, it answers the questions they may have about their condition, the treatment they're interested in, and who will be providing their care. While you may not think that your patients would be interested in something like a staff biography, it turns out that they vastly prefer content of that nature to anything that looks like an ad. Above all, readers will be drawn to informational content that helps them make decisions about their medical care.

Your content should humanize your practice, help patients understand conditions and injuries, and put them at ease about visiting your office. At the same time, remember to avoid giving specific medical advice online unless you've checked with your lawyer; even answering questions posted in the comments of a blog post with medical advice can turn into a legal issue – save that conversation for an in-office visit.

HOW TO GET STARTED WITH CONTENT MARKETING

DEVELOPING A CONTENT CALENDAR

The key to producing consistent content is to plan ahead of time. One of the best ways to make sure you publish regularly is to create a monthly or quarterly content calendar to keep your content marketing on target. Your calendar can include social media posts, email blasts, blog updates, and other types of content you think your audience might find valuable.

A content calendar maps out what posts you will publish over the next several weeks or months. It outlines the topics to be delivered, touchpoints for each post, the keyword focus (if any), due dates, and who is assigned to write individual pieces of content. Your content calendar can stretch as far into the future as you want, but keep in mind that trending topics will change rapidly. It's therefore best to restrict your calendar somewhat, and not plan further ahead than a month or two.

To start with, find a calendar that works for you. If you're a paper and pen person, an old school desk calendar works just as well as online calendars. The WordPress Editorial Calendar plugin offers a more integrated approach, allowing you to draft articles directly on your calendar.

Once you've found a good calendar, determine what your content marketing will look like. It may be helpful to craft a mission statement that defines what types of content you'll publish and outlines some of your goals. The best goals are those that are attainable and measurable, like scheduling a certain number of appointments through your website per month.

TOPIC DEVELOPMENT

The next step in creating your content calendar is nailing down a list of topics to write about. A couple questions to bear in mind when considering potential topics:

- Is it relevant? One reason narrowing down your target audience is so important is because it will help you choose topics that they can relate to. For instance, a senior citizen with back pain wouldn't be interested in articles about how jogging relieves stress, while a 30-year-old marathoner would. This is why it's important to know which patients you truly want to serve. If you serve a variety of patients, be prepared to create content that speaks to them all.

- Is it directed at your audience? Your blog should cover topics that your audience will be interested in reading. Much of what you post will center on medical topics, but it's also a good idea to post about local events, like a charity cookout or a little league game. Lighten up your informational medical content with content that touches your patients' daily lives.

Brainstorming new topics to write about can be exhausting. Tools like BuzzSumo or Google Keyword Planner are helpful in coming up with multiple topics.

Buzzsumo, for instance, tracks popular articles online. Type in a general topic, like carpal tunnel, and Buzzsumo will generate a list of popular related content. Google Keyword Planner can also help generate new topics. Typing in one keyword will prompt Keyword Planner to display a list of similar keywords. For instance, the keyword phrase "hand pain" generates other topics like "surgery carpal" and "symptoms carpal." Some of those would have to be broken down into subtopics, but you could write a good blog post on common symptoms of carpal tunnel or on the different types of surgeries available to treat it.

Both of these tools can help you brainstorm a list of topics to include on your calendar. Other good places to look for trending topics are social media platforms, like Twitter, Facebook, and Reddit. You can also brainstorm topics by recalling questions patients have asked in your office – "Frequently Asked Questions" articles would be helpful to all of your patients. Plus, once they're written, you can refer patients to your online articles to help answer some of the questions they may pose to you over the internet.

Simply put, start writing about the conditions, injuries, and treatments your practice has expertise in and can help with. Once that's complete, look into writing about what patients should expect when visiting your office(s) and your practice philosophy. Build factual pages about each, and soon, you'll be on your way to creating your own medical content library. This will serve as an invaluable resource to draw upon for deploying content in the mediums you choose to leverage, which can include blogs, social media platforms, eNewsletters, instructional articles, eBooks, infographics, podcasts, videos, webinars, and whitepapers.

OPTIMIZING YOUR CONTENT MARKETING EFFORTS

After you've created a topic list, assign those topics a publication date on your content calendar. Remember to put seasonal or holiday-related topics in the appropriate months. Don't overload yourself by trying to schedule a post every single day unless you're sure you can do it. Writing thorough blog posts is hard work and may take more time than you have. One well-written post is better than five poorly-written posts. Check out your competitors to see how much they post. If they post irregularly or rarely, you're already a step ahead by publishing content once a week; if they post more often, you will probably want to match their output.

Start off by scheduling posts once a week or even once a month. If you have more time, you can always ramp up the number of posts you publish later. One way to increase your content output is to ask your peers to guest post on your blog. This will give them added publicity and credibility, as well as take some of the pressure to create content off of your shoulders.

BLOGGING BEST PRACTICES

When it comes to content marketing by blogging, your goal should be to engage your audience. To do so, here are some best practices to follow.

BE AUTHENTIC

The internet is a crowded space, and you're competing for your patients' attention with their favorite celebrities, their friends, and every possible brand out there. Being true to yourself sets you apart from the crowd. Putting a human element into your blogging makes you more trustworthy and helps your patients relate to you. Your patients will see right through any lack of authenticity, and they are more likely to engage with you if they sense that you are being honest.

So how do you come across as authentic to faceless readers? First, listen. It all starts by listening to what your patients have to say in your office and online. What are they struggling with? What do they need to hear? Empathize with them by showing that you not only understand where they are coming from, but that you know how to help them.

Don't be afraid to be passionate. Share causes you care about, and take a stand. For instance, if you believe a certain treatment does more harm than good, don't be wishy-washy. Say what you think and explain why.

Keep your messaging consistent, both on and offline. Your voice on your blog should be consistent with what patients hear when they visit your office or talk to you on the phone.

BE EDUCATIONAL

Educate your patients on issues that are important to them. If you cater to athletes in their thirties, you could write a post on how to avoid injuries as the body ages. If you cater to older patients, they might appreciate articles that provide tips on how to avoid common bone or muscle ailments, or information about osteoporosis treatment. You can also include informational articles on popular medicines or current events happening in the medical world that are receiving mainstream media coverage, and about which patients may be curious to learn more.

USE VISUALS

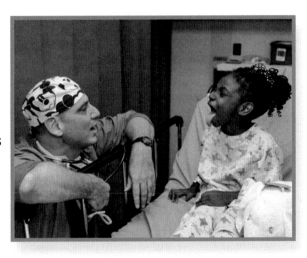

Using color images in your posts will increase the likelihood that your audience will actually read your post instead of scrolling past it. Visuals help grab your reader's attention and engage them in what you are reading. A blog post on arthritis, for example, could include images showing the difference between an arthritic knee and a healthy knee. A post on how to protect muscles while lifting weights could include a graph showing the percentage of athletes who injure themselves. Using original images is also a great way to get backlinks to your site. Since colleges, universities, and other third parties are frequently looking to reference authentic images of conditions, injuries, and treatments on their own sites, providing images in your content will encourage these institutions to link back to your site, thereby improving your search rankings.

BE RESPONSIVE

Once your posts start garnering some traffic, your readers will start commenting on your articles. Some comments will be positive, others will ask for more information, and you can count on some negative ones as well.

Be quick to respond to negative comments. Show respect to the commenter, acknowledge their point of view, and ask questions to find out where they're coming from. If necessary, don't be afraid to ask to move the conversation to a more private platform.

For example, if a reader left a comment stating that a treatment you listed for arthritis didn't work when he tried it, your response could look something like this:

"Hi Joe, thanks for reading and commenting! I'm sorry to hear that the treatment was ineffective. Can you send me an email to explain a little more about your treatment? I've found that in the majority of to most of my patients."

Similar to responding to negative patient reviews, the best thing to do is to take the high road and work offline to rectify the situation, if required.

Responding to comments can be time consuming, but it's an important part of blogging. Your audience needs to know that this post is just the start of the conversation. Engaging patients in the comments could eventually lead to them coming to your office.

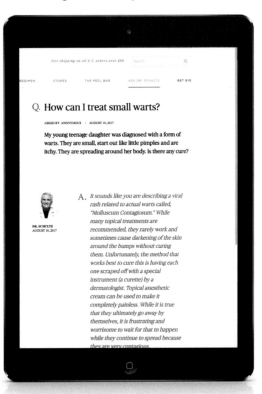

PROMOTE

Unless you actively promote your blog, few people will ever read it.

Work to build relationships with other doctors in your field who are bloggers to cross-promote each other's posts. When you do your topic research, you'll find other sources who have written similar material –

share your articles with them in hopes that they will in turn share it with their networks.

Share every article on your social media accounts as well, and use a tool like MailChimp or ConstantContact to email your posts to your patients every month. Also, consider reaching out to colleagues and influencers in your field to ask them to share your posts. Finally, plan to re-share your posts throughout the year, repurposing them if necessary.

This may all seem overwhelming, but it doesn't have to be. Pick a few mediums most applicable to your practice, and branch out over time. The benefits of sharing consistent content don't happen overnight, but they compound in value as time goes on. As medical content marketing adoption continues, you want to be securely positioned in your niche market.

Consider these three statistics:

- 77 percent of internet health searches begin at an internet search engine like Google, Yahoo, or Bing. (Pew Research Center)
- 74 percent of consumers say they prefer to get information about a company through a series of articles, rather than ads. (Content Marketing Institute)
- 61 percent of consumers say they feel better about a company after reading custom content. (Content Marketing Institute)

These numbers are rising every year, meaning content marketing is here to stay in health care. *Your content marketing strategy could be the difference between finding new patients and expanding, or losing patients and stagnating.* By delivering consistent content in a professional, people-oriented, and conversational tone, readers will begin establishing a professional and emotional connection with you.

Creating an integrated digital content library for your practice gives you the powerful motor needed to drive patient acquisition and retention, increase traffic to your website, and improve your professional reputation.

BUILDING AUTHORITY WITH CONSISTENT CONTENT CHECKLIST:

- ☐ Determine the medium(s) most applicable to your practice.
- ☐ Develop your practice's brand voice.
- ☐ Develop a content calendar to organize the publication of your content.
- ☐ Generate a list of topics about which to write.
- ☐ Write in a simple, conversational, people-oriented tone.
- ☐ Focus on one topic per content piece.
- ☐ Do not continually write about how great your practice is.
- ☐ Use targeted keywords (terms patients are familiar with) in your messaging to increase search engine rankings.
- ☐ Deliver your content on a consistent basis.
- ☐ Create relevant links from your articles to other pages on your site for greater search engine visibility.
- ☐ Periodically sharing relevant third-party articles is okay; share valuable, relevant information that aims to solve the specific needs of patients.
- ☐ Respond to comments, both positive and negative.
- ☐ Promote your content, through social media, email, and shares on other websites.

CHAPTER 8

COMMUNICATING AND EDUCATING WITH EMAIL MARKETING

With 4.3 billion global users, email has become almost as ubiquitous as the internet itself. According to the email marketing firm ExactTarget, over 91 percent of all American adults check their email accounts every day – that's only slightly behind the 98 percent who check their physical mailbox on a daily basis, as reported by the US Postal Service. Email is also popular with patients; according to a report by Merkle, 74 percent of patients said they prefer to receive commercial communications through email rather than through direct mail.

Yet, despite the universality, popularity, and age of email (which has existed in some form since the earliest days of the internet), many medical practitioners still haven't embraced it in the same manner as their patients. A 2015 Nielsen survey commissioned by the Council of Accountable Physician Practices and the Bipartisan Policy Center demonstrated that the majority of health and medical providers in the United States are still not using email to communicate with their patients – in any form.

Given the so-far limited embrace of email by medical practitioners, it's no wonder that most are missing out on the benefits of using email to promote their practices. After reading this chapter, you will not only be able to take full advantage of the opportunities presented by email marketing, but will find yourself ahead of many of your peers in the health care industry.

WHAT IS EMAIL MARKETING?

Regardless of where you currently land on the email adoption curve, it's important to understand that *email marketing is currently the easiest and least costly way for you to market yourself and your practice*. It's also well within the capability and budget of even the smallest practices.

Email marketing, as used by a medical practice, can take numerous forms. These can include pre-appointment reminders (to decrease your no-show rate), promotional newsletters designed to sell new services, post-surgery information, and recovery guidelines aimed at reinforcing instructions given to patients during their appointments. Recurring communications can also be easily automated with software systems, making email marketing an important channel for health care providers who are interested in improving both patient experience and practice efficiency.

As email continues to play an increasingly important role in the lives of current and future patients, the best practices are taking full advantage of all the benefits email marketing has to offer. For example, if you're a chiropractor, dentist, dermatologist, or therapist – someone who sees patients on a frequent basis (or numerous times over the course of their lives) – there's no better marketing channel than email to keep your patients aware, engaged, and returning to your practice. Email marketing is also great for general and family practices, where it can be used as an effective way to stay top-of-mind with patients who are increasingly turning to Urgent Care clinics for care they could easily be receiving from a general practitioner.

WHY YOUR PRACTICE SHOULD USE EMAIL MARKETING

Beyond the basic fact that email is quick, easy, and popular with patients, it also allows you to save time on certain patient communications and set yourself apart from your competition, all at a lower cost than other marketing channels. So, really, why wouldn't you take advantage of email marketing?

AUTOMATING ALERTS, COMMUNICATIONS, AND REMINDERS

Regardless of your specialty or practice type, time is your biggest constraint; you can never seem to have enough of it. There's always something new added to your to-do list, which often causes other tasks to fall by the wayside. Frequently, it's your marketing that suffers.

Rest assured, *with email marketing, time is not an issue.* That's because one of the benefits of using email is the ability to automate all sorts of internal and external communications. Appointment reminders, post-visit review solicitations, and informational surveys can all be automatically sent to your patients via email with low-cost, readily available software services. You can also utilize email to alert you to certain events, such as the posting of a new review to one of your online profiles.

These types of emails are not always thought of as email marketing because they're not promotional in nature, but they are, in fact, major components of any practice's email marketing efforts. An automated sequence of emails can create a valuable feedback loop between you and your patients, which will improve both their in-practice experience and their overall health outcomes. For example, automated email sequences can be used in the days prior to a prospective patient's first appointment, to show them the benefits they will receive by working with you. When combined with appointment reminders, these emails are virtually certain to dramatically reduce your no-show rate. You can also use automated email sequences to send post-surgery or post-treatment instructions to patients at key milestones in their recovery process. Once you create and set up the campaign, emails will be sent for as long as you keep the program activated, freeing you up to focus on more of what you love – seeing patients.

EFFECTIVELY CUT THROUGH ONLINE NOISE

You're not the only one fighting for the attention of internet users. Your competitors are also interested in getting in front of your current and prospective patients, on both search engines and social media.

Think about it. Search Google, what do you see? Ads. Scroll down your Facebook feed, what do you see? Ads. This is the same thing that your patients see, all day, every day. Ads on ads on ads. No wonder it's so hard to generate awareness for your practice.

This creates email's biggest advantage – direct access. Email provides a direct communication channel to your patients, an effective one-to-one interface that cuts through the advertising clutter and marketing noise that they are often bombarded with when they search online or reach out for a recommendation on social media. Since you already have your patients' email addresses, you've overcome the two biggest challenges of marketing – awareness and attention – without even trying. Your patients are obviously already aware that you and your practice exist, and they've given you permission to email them. Therefore, when an email from you hits their inbox, it's likely to get their attention immediately.

Whether or not they take action will depend on your targeting, content, and calls-to-action, something we will discuss later in this chapter.

THE LOWEST COST MARKETING CHANNEL

There are a number of channels available for marketing your practice online. In a perfect world, you could use all of them to drive patient acquisition, improve your professional reputation, and manage patient retention. In reality, however, you and your practice operate on a budget, which has to be taken into account when making marketing decisions.

That's one of the biggest advantages of email marketing – it doesn't cost a lot. In fact, in many cases, sending a monthly email newsletter to your patients could cost you nothing more than your time. *Email marketing is the lowest cost marketing channel, and will therefore result in some of the highest return on investment.*

Email is low cost for a number of reasons. First, quite simply, it's fairly cheap to send digital information across the internet. Second, you already own the most important element (your patients' email addresses). Third, thanks to automation and reusable templates, it requires much less human effort over time; once your email marketing strategy is underway it largely runs by itself and necessitates very little further monetary investment.

Email marketing is also a low cost way to complement or replace direct mail campaigns. This is because many of the most frequent forms of email for medical practices – announcements, coupons, deals, and offers – are also the core of effective direct mail. Sending this material to your existing (and potential) patients through email can either further reinforce what your practice is already sending via direct mail, or replace direct mail altogether with a lower cost alternative.

TYPES OF EMAIL MARKETING

As we've touched on already, there are numerous ways to market your practice using email. The most common, of course, takes the form of a newsletter. The email newsletter has become – outside of individual patient communications – the poster child for email marketing within health and medical practices. Email newsletters, sent en masse to current or prospective patients, come in three main forms: educational, informational, and promotional. It's important to consider which form will be most effective for your practice before you start sending any bulk newsletter communications.

EDUCATIONAL EMAIL NEWSLETTERS

Considering all of the complaints by health and medical practitioners about the likes of WebMD and other health information outlets, most practices would be well-served by turning to email in order to educate their patients.

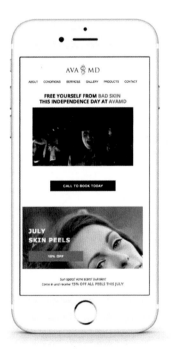

Educational email newsletters offer an opportunity for you to update your patients on current health trends that have hit the news, seasonal health-related items, and other, more pointed information on new health concerns or threats that come within your area of expertise. The goal of these newsletters is not to sell a product or your practice, but instead to educate your patients, ideally on a consistent, monthly basis. That being said, receiving accurate, health-related knowledge from you and your practice helps brand you as an expert and keeps your practice top-of-mind, should a patient have need of your services.

INFORMATIONAL EMAIL NEWSLETTERS

Educational emails are an excellent way to keep your patient-base engaged, but there is a great deal of other information patients find relevant that you may not be sending them.

Informational emails, typically sent on a more ad hoc basis than educational newsletters, offer you and your practice the opportunity to make your patients aware of any important operational matters affecting their care. Whether that involves announcing a new practitioner, unveiling new locations, or providing updates to policies and procedures, informational email newsletters are an effective complement to offline communication strategies.

The goal of these informational emails is to cut through all the other messages that your patients are hit with every day, allowing them to keep up with the changes to, and growth of, your practice.

PROMOTIONAL EMAIL NEWSLETTERS

Last, but certainly not least, is the promotional newsletter. The most well-known and heavily used of the three email newsletters amongst health and medical practices, promotional newsletters are your own private HSN or QVC. With promotional newsletters, you can showcase new products and services available at your practice, or offer coupons, discounts, and other deals.

Despite their popularity, promotional newsletters also get the most scrutiny from practitioners and patients. As a result, the use of promotional email newsletters is not for every practice (i.e. most patients aren't holding off on a hip replacement until they see a 15 percent off coupon from their orthopedic surgeon). If you do decide to send promotional newsletters, they should be used sparingly, limited to one per month unless patients have specifically asked to receive them more often. After all, the goal of your promotional email efforts is to drive new patient visits and increase revenue, not lose them with an annoying deluge of advertisements.

BEYOND NEWSLETTERS: OTHER USES FOR EMAIL MARKETING

Email newsletters are the most well-known and utilized form of email marketing, but they are just the beginning. Email can be used to help market your practice in a number of other less obvious, but nonetheless important, ways. Today, software systems exist that leverage email to automate alerts and communications that are often forgotten or overlooked by practice staff.

PATIENT APPOINTMENT REMINDERS

No-shows cost health care clinics billions each year. Worldwide studies concerning the prevalence of patient no-shows vary, but it's estimated that between 15 percent and 30 percent of all patients never arrive to their appointment.

That's where email comes in.

While patients tend to slightly prefer text message appointment reminders, sending appointment reminders by email is an effective way to decrease patient no-shows and increase your bottom line. Software systems exist that can integrate with your existing electronic health records (EHR), electronic medical records (EMR), and scheduling system to send automated emails (and text messages) to patients ahead of appointments. A study by the Journal of Telemedicine and Telecare reported that patient no-shows were reduced by almost a third when an automated patient reminder system was used.

How much extra revenue does that add up to for you?

PATIENT REVIEW SOLICITATION

Improving your bottom line isn't only about ensuring all your patients show up for appointments. In order to grow your practice, you also need to develop a sterling online reputation, as has already been discussed. One way that you can help improve your online reputation is with automated patient review solicitations.

The same software that can generate patient appointment reminders can also be used to send automated emails to your patients after they visit your practice. While some practitioners may be worried about the downsides of proactively soliciting reviews on their public online profiles, technology can be used to help minimize those concerns. Some software, such as InboundMD and RepCheckup, uses a two-step process to first verify that a particular patient has had a positive experience, and then urge him or her to leave a positive review on one of your review site profiles.

Sending automated emails to patients soliciting reviews will enhance your online reputation and help lower the potential impact of the negative reviews that inevitably occur.

PATIENT EXPERIENCE AND SATISFACTION SURVEYS

Email can be used to improve more than just your bottom line. It can also be used to gain insight into your patients' experiences with your practice.

Utilizing email, you can create an automated patient experience feedback process. Sending automated patient experience and satisfaction surveys allows you to learn what your practice is doing well and where it needs to improve. This creates a perfect feedback loop for practitioners, practice managers, and staff, allowing opportunities for positive change to surface more quickly.

As with patient reminders and review solicitations, software exists that integrates directly with your EHR/EMR that, once configured, makes this feedback loop simple to initiate and operate. With the shift toward a value-based health care system, soliciting this information has become an important part of improving your patients' in-office experience and maximizing your practice's bottom line.

DRIP MARKETING

While some of these types of email marketing may be new to you, the reality is that they aren't exactly cutting edge. In fact, most of the email marketing strategies and tactics described here have been used by health and medical practices for more than a decade. There is one emerging area of email marketing that not all practitioners have harnessed, however. That's drip marketing.

What is drip marketing? Drip marketing refers to a marketing campaign that features an automated sequence of pre-written emails on a particular subject that are sent over a period of time to an interested person. For example, let's say you're a reproductive endocrinologist and your fertility clinic is having trouble getting prospective patients who requested an appointment online to actually *schedule* an appointment. You can use a drip marketing campaign to send an automated sequence of emails to those patients. These emails would focus on introducing you and the practice, detailing what patients can expect when coming to the clinic, providing information about your success rates, and offering up stories from actual patients you've helped, all with the goal of motivating the patient to take the next step and schedule an appointment to see you.

Side note: While drip marketing campaigns most often take the form of a series of emails, they can also incorporate text messages, postcards, and even phone calls.

This is also an effective way to maximize your front office staff's efforts when it comes to booking new patient appointments. With a drip campaign in place, you can reduce the time your front office staff might be spending calling or emailing patients back manually.

Another example of drip marketing would be an automated sequence of emails sent post-procedure or post-treatment, reinforcing the recovery instructions and/or plan. This is an effective way for orthopedic surgeons, orthodontists, and physical therapists to complement in-clinic and take-home reference materials. In this scenario, the patient would receive an email at corresponding points in the recovery process, maybe once per week for the entire six week recovery period, reinforcing rehabilitation and/or rest protocols. You could also include generalized information about how the patient should be feeling or the approximate range of motion they should have at any given time, with a note to call the clinic if their recovery seems to be proceeding at a slower pace than expected.

As is true with all of the other methods outlined above, software does exist to help you implement drip marketing, but you should be advised that these particular campaigns tend to be more involved (and time-consuming) than other methods of email marketing. Depending on how busy you are with your practice, you might want to consider bringing in an outside expert to help implement your drip marketing strategy.

THE DOS AND DON'TS OF EMAIL MARKETING

Hopefully by now you're excited to begin or expand your email marketing efforts.

After all, we've seen that email is:

- Low cost, especially compared to other types of marketing
- An attractive way to communicate with patients
- Easily automated and integrated with your other practice systems
- Proven to be effective at driving action and conversions

Before you roll up your sleeves and jump in at the deep end, however, here's a PSA: email marketing is part art and part science. This means that there's a lot of nuance when it comes to what constitutes effective usage of email. You might think you're doing it right, but you could just as easily be doing it all wrong. To help guide your email marketing success, consider the following Dos and Don'ts.

THE DOS OF EMAIL MARKETING

DO make sure your email data is accurate. You'll never reach a patient via email if the email address you have on file for him or her is incorrect. You also won't win any friends by calling Frank, "Hank." If you're going to effectively use email marketing, you will need to make sure your email list and patient data is accurate, even if this requires frequent, manual review. This is especially important if you're using code in your email templates that culls information (first names, for example) directly from your email list.

DO get permission before emailing patients. While the majority of your patients use email daily, not all of them want to hear from you through that medium. Prior to sending a patient anything via email, make sure you've received their permission to do so. A great way to do this is to add a small section to your intake forms allowing patients to select their communications preferences.

DO have a compelling email subject line. The email subject is the first thing a patient will read and thus plays an important role in whether the rest of the message will be read. For those patients who regularly receive a high volume of emails, a strong subject line will help you stand out from everything else that they receive on a given day. Strive to be as concise as possible while still remaining descriptive about the rest of the email's contents.

DO personalize the email. As mentioned above, you can often insert code that allows you to pull particular data about a patient from your records and insert it into the email. This type of personalization aides in improving the overall tone of the email, as it makes it seem more human. After all, patients, as people, ultimately want to hear from another person, not a machine.

DO include a main call-to-action. Your email marketing efforts will only be successful if you have a clear call-to-action (CTA) for patients to take when receiving your communication. Your calls-to-action should be simple, such as "Schedule an Appointment Now," or "Buy Now" if you're featuring a new product for patients to purchase. When in doubt, it's better to be direct than creative when it comes to your CTAs.

DO be mobile-friendly. As has been discussed in previous chapters, patients are using their mobile phones more and more every year. This makes designing (and writing) for mobile devices an important "do" when it comes to email marketing. Ensuring that your email templates are optimized for mobile phones (make sure you check before sending) and that you're being concise in your writing (without sacrificing comprehension) are two effective ways to make sure patients on-the-go will click on your message.

DO include a link to unsubscribe. While many patients do want to receive your emails, others will decide to opt out of your messaging. That's why it's critical (and also legally required, in order to comply with the CAN-SPAM Act) to include a link to unsubscribe in every bulk communication sent to a patient. This is required regardless of whether or not a particular patient originally signed up to receive the communication. Also, be prepared for patients to reach out to you asking to unsubscribe, without using the "Unsubscribe" link. Yes, it's frustrating, but it happens.

Pro Tip: Offer patients the ability to choose which emails they receive. Oftentimes, patients feel overwhelmed by the number of commercial messages they receive, but still want to get your educational newsletters. Offering them the ability, upon both initial sign-up and the "Unsubscribe" page, to choose which communications they wish to receive (or continue to receive) is a great way to improve your patients' email experience while keeping your email list growing.

DO send a test email before sending a bulk communication. It may seem like a no-brainer, but we at InboundMD witness email misfires all the time. You should always send out a test email prior to sending your mass communications. In fact, we recommend that you send your test emails out to a few people, even to some that are outside of your own practice, in order to find errors and issues. At a minimum, try to have three different sets of eyes review your email.

THE DON'TS OF EMAIL MARKETING

DON'T send marketing emails using "CC" or "BCC" fields. When it comes to sending bulk or mass email messages to your patients, never use the CC or BCC fields. This is the entire reason email marketing software exists in the first place. Your email recipients hate receiving these types of communications, especially if their email address is exposed to others. Depending on the content of the email, this could even become a HIPAA (Health Insurance Portability and Accountability Act) violation for you and your practice.

DON'T send more than one email per week. Remember, you're not the only professional reading about sending emails to consumers. Your patients *are* consumers, and they are likely getting emails from many different companies and service providers throughout the day, week, and month. Many will get email fatigue, so from both a branding and effectiveness standpoint, avoid sending more than one email per week. Even this might be too much – for most practices, just one email a month can deliver great results.

DON'T give specific medical advice. As with all of the information you distribute online, when it comes to email marketing, you have to be careful about what you send to patients. To be safe, ensure that any bulk or mass email messaging does not contain specific medical advice or any claims that could be in violation of the law. It's probably not necessary to involve your lawyer in every message, but being mindful of this issue as you craft your email communications will help keep you safe.

DON'T reveal protected health information (PHI).

This is a big one, and it's part of the reason you should never use CC or BCC fields. When it comes to email marketing, you have to protect PHI, so unless you've received written permission from a patient beforehand, never mention or reference a specific patient, their condition, or their treatment in your emails. If you're unsure about whether an email that you are composing might be revealing PHI, err on the side of caution. Consult your lawyer or simply don't include the material you think might be inappropriate.

DON'T forget HIPAA compliance. Next to accidentally or inadvertently revealing PHI, a data breach that would expose patient information to the world should be your next biggest concern. This means that you should ensure that your email marketing service complies with HIPAA protocols. Have any outside contractors you bring in to help with your email marketing campaign sign a business associate agreement (BAA), if you can.

DON'T forget to review the results. Sure, email is one of the easiest and most effective channels there is for marketing your practice, but that doesn't mean that your efforts don't need to be optimized over time. As you implement and grow your usage of email marketing, make sure to take the time to review the results of each campaign. Understanding your open, click-through, and conversion rates will allow you to tweak future campaigns, maximizing your results. This topic will be discussed further in Chapter 11.

ANATOMY OF AN EMAIL NEWSLETTER

Email newsletters can come in a variety of shapes and sizes, and can employ a multitude of different colors and fonts. In contrast to these variations, *however, the underlying structure of almost every well-produced, effective email newsletter is comprised of the same elements.*

These elements may seem mundane at first glance, and you're likely already familiar with most of them. It's nonetheless worth revisiting them since, as you well know, a routine checkup is never a bad thing.

"From field"

Subject line

Body

Content headers

Content

Footer

Unsubscribe   Social Sharing

THE "FROM" FIELD

As the name suggests, the "From" field is used to show an email recipient the identity of the person sending them the email. As we suggested earlier when discussing personalization, you should make sure that the name used in the "From" field is that of a person. It can be your own name or that of another practitioner with whom you work, but try to avoid using the name of the practice. Remember, patients are people, and people want to interact with other people.

SUBJECT LINE

Together with the "From" field, the subject line gives patients the biggest indication of what an email is about – and the motivation to open it. When writing subject lines, it's important to consider length (shorter is typically better) and to avoid any words that might trigger a recipient's spam filters (for example, "free," "coupon," or "deal," among others). You can also personalize the subject lines if you wish: "Hi {Insert First Name}, thank you for contacting us!"

BODY

If the "From" field and subject line are a taste of what's to come in an email, the body is the main course. The body of your email should contain a number of items, from compelling headers to calls-to-action. Depending on the type of newsletter you're sending, the nature of these body elements may change; to decide exactly what form your body elements should take, consider the audience for whom you're writing and what action you want them to take.

CONTENT HEADERS

In our fast-paced, always-on-the-scroll world, headers help make sure your message sticks (or at least keep your patients scrolling down for more). Your email newsletter should have at least one compelling header, often used as the lead-in that serves as an overview of the email's contents. If you're covering a lot of ground, it's okay to use multiple headers to break up sections of content.

CONTENT

The content of your email can take many different forms, from text and images to videos or even a GIF. What's important to remember about content is that brevity is key, especially since your email has a high probability of being read on a mobile phone. Try to avoid long paragraphs and sentences, which often make things tougher to read, in favor of paragraphs of two to three sentences and bulleted lists. Additionally, be sure to lace your newsletters with different calls-to-action (CTAs) that ask readers to take a specific action, such as "Liking" your Facebook page, scheduling an appointment, or taking advantage of a promotion.

FOOTER

A footer comes after the email content, in which you should include social sharing buttons, links, and contact information for the practice. It's best not to get too fancy with the footer and just stick to the basics. After all, your goal should be to have patients follow a link or call-to-action within the content section of the email, before they even see the footer.

UNSUBSCRIBE

The "Unsubscribe" link, mandatory for all bulk or mass email communications to patients, is also found in the footer. Make sure each of your bulk email communications includes an "Unsubscribe" link.

SOCIAL SHARING

The last, but certainly not least, important part of an email newsletter is the social sharing buttons or links. Depending on your specialty, patients may be willing to share your educational and or promotional newsletters with their friends and families on social networks, furthering your reach. Including links to promote the newsletter via major social networks should be a part of every email message you send.

HOW TO CREATE A BASIC EMAIL MARKETING CAMPAIGN FOR YOUR PRACTICE

Finally, once you know how to construct an effective email newsletter and what you should and shouldn't be putting into your email communications, it's time to bring everything together and come up with a plan for how you can implement an effective email marketing campaign – in any of the forms we've covered in this chapter. Even if your practice is already sending email newsletters to patients, this section will serve as a refresher and offer new ideas to enhance your existing efforts.

1. **Assign a point person.** Whether it's you, your practice manager, or even your in-house marketer, in order to be successful with email marketing there needs to be a point person to oversee and coordinate your efforts. This is true even if you outsource your production to an agency or a freelancer.

2. Collect (and clean up) your patients' emails. You won't be able to take advantage of the benefits of email personalization (or even reach your patients, for that matter) if you have poor data. Before you get started, spend some time going through your data to ensure that it's clean and accurate.

3. Determine your topics and publishing schedule. Email marketing is not a one-time event. It's something that needs to be done consistently in order to stay top-of-mind with patients and ensure high engagement with the messages you send. Creating a content calendar, whether it extends for three months or a year, is a great way to organize and plan your efforts.

4. Select your email marketing software. With good data and a

plan in place, you can now select an email marketing software program to power your campaign. There are dozens of major providers, all of which offer free accounts to those with a small number of email addresses in their list. MailChimp is a great service to start with, but you should check out a few others to determine which will best suit the needs of you and your practice.

5. Create your email content. Now that you've got your email marketing software up and running, it's time to write your email content. Doing this before you move on to designing and building the email itself will not only save you time but also allow the design of the email to fit its message, making for a more professional presentation.

6. Design and format your email. Once you're happy with your email's content, you can design the final version using your email marketing software. Your email marketing program should have plenty of tools to make your message look professional and aesthetically pleasing. Most software packages come with pre-existing templates from which you can directly copy and paste, as well as more barebones options, for those creative practitioners who want to have a go at building a unique email template from scratch.

7. Send your test version. You should never forget to send a test version of your email (or two, or three). It's very easy to overlook a mistake you've made, so having a few more eyes inspect your work helps ensure that everything is correct before any patients see it. Misspellings and broken links are the two most commonly found errors in email newsletters, so pay the most attention to those areas.

8. Publish your email. Once your final draft is tested and loaded into your email marketing software, you're just about ready to hit "Send." Before you do, however, give some thought to *when* you want patients to receive your communications. Most email

marketing software allows you to schedule your emails to be sent at a specific date and time. Take advantage of this functionality – sending an email right after you finish it at 1 a.m. on a Saturday night isn't likely to bring you the best results.

9. **Review your results.** Speaking of results, don't forget to review them! About a week or so after your first campaign, set aside fifteen or thirty minutes to review the results. Pay attention to the open, click-through, and conversion rates. If you're trying to sell a specific product, you can also check out the revenue generated from the campaign. Use what you learn during your review to improve your future campaigns. If and when you get more advanced with your email marketing efforts, you can use your results as part of more involved A/B split testing efforts.

Email marketing is the easiest and most cost-effective way to market both your skills and your practice, and is especially useful for practitioners with limited marketing resources. Whether you decide to stick with the basics and only send one email to your patients per month or to fully embrace email and communicate with your patients for the entirety of their individual journeys with you, there's no denying that every practice should be taking advantage of the many benefits that come with email marketing.

EMAIL MARKETING CHECKLIST:

☐ Implement email sign-up subscription forms on each practice website.

☐ Implement email sign-up subscription forms on each practice's social media profiles.

☐ Ask patients for permission to send them email communications on your in-practice forms.

☐ Ensure existing email data is up-to-date and otherwise accurate.

☐ Develop a content calendar and publishing schedule for your email marketing.

☐ Implement email marketing software.

☐ Send out email newsletters on a consistent basis.

☐ Use personalized messaging with the patient's name in your correspondences.

☐ Keep subject lines and messaging copy short, simple, and to the point.

☐ Be sure to use spell check.

☐ Include clear, strong CTAs in all of your email marketing material.

☐ Design responsive email templates for your practice.

☐ Conduct research on optimal days/times to deploy your emails.

☐ Send a few test emails to ensure that all links and content displays correctly.

☐ Make sure your email marketing is mobile-friendly.

☐ Stay in compliance with HIPAA and the CAN-SPAM Act.

☐ Automate the sending of patient appointment reminders, review solicitations, and post-treatment follow-up instructions.

☐ Monitor email subscribes and unsubscribes.

☐ Analyze email metrics and iterate your strategy accordingly.

CHAPTER 9

ENGAGING WITH PATIENTS ON SOCIAL MEDIA

With a search engine optimized website, accurate local listings, reputation monitoring in place, and an email marketing strategy, your next step is to harness the power of engaging with patients and targeting them through advertising on relevant social media channels.

According to a PwC Health Research Institute survey, around 40 percent of people use social media when researching a health care provider. While the majority of patients are not going straight to social media for help with their health care needs yet, social networks like Facebook, Twitter, and YouTube play a role in approximately one-third of searches for medical information. Among patients between the ages of eighteen and twenty-four, a full 90 percent turn to social media to find medical information.

Even though social media has been characterized as something only the young have embraced, older patients are also increasingly making use of social platforms. While younger generations do adapt to social networks more quickly, usage of social platforms by senior citizens has tripled in the last six years, according to a Pew study. In the past ten years, the majority of adults have started using one form of social media or another, meaning health care providers no longer have any excuse for not including social media as part of their practice marketing mix.

WHY USE SOCIAL MEDIA?

Personal referrals have long been the lifeblood of any medical practice. It should come as no surprise that patients prefer the opinions of their social groups to the advertising and marketing they're inundated with on a daily basis. The challenge that many health care providers face today, however, is in recognizing that the process of gaining word-of-mouth referrals has changed.

Today, *social media is the new word-of-mouth marketing.* People are no longer restricted to asking close friends or family for medical referrals. Increasingly, they're going online to see what other people have to say on social media, casting a much wider net for feedback and recommendations.

Here are the numbers, according to data compiled by The Spark Report, a publication focused on advertising and marketing:

- 46 percent of patients trust health-related social media content shared by patients they know; 25 percent said they also trust the content shared by patients they don't know.

- 42 percent of patients said that they would share a positive experience with their doctor online, and 35 percent said that they would share their negative experiences.

- 41 percent of surveyed patients said that social media content influences their decisions regarding doctors, hospitals, or other medical facilities.

As patients become increasingly comfortable discussing their personal health online, these percentages are sure to grow, especially since it is so easy to turn to social media for medical referrals. It's worth keeping in mind that as younger patients age, the social networks that they have become accustomed to using to communicate with their friends will naturally become one of their preferred methods of interaction with their health care providers as an adult. As time goes on, therefore, social media will become increasingly important to your practice.

This data also suggests that the reach of word-of-mouth medical referrals has grown exponentially with social media. In other words, the geographical scope of your potential referral market has expanded. Traditional word-of-mouth relied on physical proximity, between parents with children attending the same school or among families worshipping at the same church. With social media, however, prospective patients who live within your service area don't need to have a first-degree connection with one of your patients to get drawn into an online conversation about your practice.

Even more interestingly, social media extends the reach of word-of-mouth because it doesn't even necessarily require the prospective patient to ask the question. In the old world of patient referral, a prospective patient typically had to take the initiative to ask someone for a name. With today's social media content streams, a prospective patient may see your name or practice being discussed by someone who was recently excited to check in at your location. Even if he or she is not in need of your services at that moment, this patient's exposure to your practice may prompt him or her to remember you in the future.

Social media also gives you more control over word-of-mouth. Your practice can get mentioned on social media because someone is sharing their own experience with you, or because someone is sharing content *from* you. You can also leverage your existing patients' networks of family and friends by featuring and tagging them in your social content.

Whether you create your own content or only share quality medical content from other sources via your social media profiles, you have the opportunity to become a trusted expert for patients long before they need you. In fact, the content you share on social media brings with it a high degree of authority exactly because you're the one who has shared it – 60 percent of social media users say they are most likely to trust the social media posts coming from doctors, according to PwC data.

Even more important than the ability to influence word-of-mouth, you can use social media to generate awareness for your practice, spread the word about innovative services you offer, and engage with patients about medical conditions concerning them. Social media sharing means that not only is your pool of potential referral patients growing, but the pool of people doing the referring on your behalf is growing, too.

For reference, the Mayo Clinic increased its podcast audience by 76,000 listeners once it started using social media as a promotional tool. It's not that these 76,000 new listeners will all someday need to be a patient at the Mayo Clinic; more important is the fact that the Mayo Clinic now has another 76,000 people sharing (or referring, if you will) their content with more people. Some percentage of this expanded audience will then hear about a new treatment for the first time on the podcast; if it's a treatment that a particular patient can benefit from, he or she might do a Google search for more information, and maybe even find your practice, if the procedure falls within your specialty.

Another benefit of contemporary word-of-mouth is that social media lets you hear and see what patients are saying, sometimes even as it happens (don't worry, it's less creepy than it sounds). You can set up queries in tools like Mention, Hootsuite, or RepCheckup to let you know when your name or your practice name is used by someone in a public social media post. Use these queries to hear what people have to say about you, your practice, or health care in general. This is great market research you can use in your overall marketing efforts – you now have access to these word-of-mouth transactions in real time and the ability to proactively create and participate in them thanks to social media.

GENERAL TIPS FOR SOCIAL MEDIA SUCCESS

Social media can be a powerful marketing tool for your health care practice if used correctly. Here are some things you can do to make sure your social strategy is effective:

DO provide fun and interesting information. You want to be seen as a reliable information source, sure, but that doesn't mean providing nothing but links to medical journal articles or lectures on healthy lifestyle habits. Use Twitter, Facebook, and other social media channels to share funny stories you come across (it probably goes without saying, but don't share your patients' private experiences or information without their signed permission) and quick medical facts that your patients might find surprising. Even sharing local news and personal interest stories can provide variety at the same time that they educate. Sharing news about your local sports teams or interesting articles about your region is a great way to connect with (or even flatter) your patients and build goodwill.

Just like the advice you give in the office, the information you provide via social media is much more likely to be taken to heart if it's presented in an engaging, patient-affirming way. Give them something to enjoy, and you can sneak the medical lessons in with greater ease and efficacy.

DO be authentic and personal. Just as you need to be authentic in your blog content, be yourself on social media. After all, in most cases, that's what patients are buying. Don't try to be the late-night talk show comedian if humor isn't your thing, and don't be a stodgy professor-type if that's not who you are.

Be willing to share your real self on your social pages, while remaining professional at all times. You'll come across as more honest and trustworthy if you do, and these are qualities that every patient appreciates in a health care provider.

DO use images in your posts. Content with relevant images will engage readers far more than similar content without images, and you'll easily see double the engagement on Facebook for posts with images in your audience's news feed. You don't have to be a professional photographer – you can just take pictures with your iPhone and share them. Patients are simply trying to get to know you; give them an inside look at your daily routine.

DO engage with your patients/audience. Remember, social media is the new standard in community building. It's not a one-way communication medium, where you post things and get patients in your office as a result. Patients using social networks expect to see you and hear your voice, as awkward or weird as that may make you feel. Social media is all about interaction – when someone comments on one of your posts, or asks a question, or even lodges a public complaint, don't just ignore it (and unless the complaint contains private information, don't delete it). It's important to your patients that you hear them and then respond to them on social media.

Follow the same guidelines for engagement laid out in previous sections: respond in a positive, professional, and pleasant manner, responsibly answer any questions, and steer any complaints or issues to a less public forum. If you can do all that each and every day, you'll be ahead of most of your competition.

DON'T just talk about yourself/your practice. Everything you share on social media should be relevant to your practice and your patients, but that doesn't mean it all has to be about you; in fact, most of it shouldn't be. If your Facebook page is nothing but calls for new patients, flu shot reminders, and office announcements, even your loyal patients will stop paying attention pretty quickly. Share useful information about health, your practice area, local events, and other goodies that people will enjoy even when they aren't thinking about their personal health care.

Reddit, a social media link-aggregating site and discussion community, sets a 9:1 ratio in their "Reddiquette" guide: for every one link to your own content/business, you should share nine posts that don't directly relate to your business at all. You can probably make that ratio a bit smaller on Facebook, Twitter, Instagram, and the rest, but the principle remains the same.

DON'T limit yourself to your existing fans/followers. You're not the only medical office in town, and you won't lose patients by sharing things you see on other medical practices' pages and feeds. Sharing other practices' and professionals' posts is actually a great way to encourage them to share yours and grow your social media reach. You can even reach out to other medical offices directly and inquire about co-marketing through shared social media posts.

DON'T mix your personal and professional social media accounts. This is a carryover from keeping professional distance in the real world, and should be a no-brainer. Get your patients to be fans of your professional Facebook page. Don't invite them to friend you on your personal account. Rest assured, you'll be very happy to have that distinction in place the first time you encounter a problem patient online.

WHAT SOCIAL NETWORKS SHOULD YOUR HEALTH CARE PRACTICE USE?

Does "being social" mean you have to be on every single social network?

Thankfully, the answer is no. You don't have to be on every social network, or even most of them. The fact is, social media has never been one-size-fits-all. *You need to tailor your social media approach to the practice you want to run and the patients you want to see,* just as each individual patient requires a tailored approach to their health care needs. There are really only a handful of social media sites where you're likely to see any sort of return on the time you invest, and choosing just a few of these to focus on will yield the best results.

WHAT SOCIAL NETWORKS ARE BEST FOR YOUR PRACTICE?

Not all social media platforms are created equal. Each one has different functionalities and appeals to a different audience. Therefore, before deciding which to use, determine what your goals are:

1. Do you want to connect with other doctors and medical professionals to start seeing more referrals?

2. Are you hoping for more industry influence and a larger all-around profile as a medical expert and care provider?

3. Is getting new patients through direct outreach and discussion at the top of your priority list?

Once you define your goals, you'll be able to choose the social media network(s) that can most easily give you the results you're looking for. Let's take a closer look at some of the most popular social media platforms.

FACEBOOK

Facebook is **the** social network for health care providers, regardless of their target audience. Nearly 90 percent of 18 to 29-year-olds are on Facebook, according to Pew data, as are 84 percent of those aged 30 to 49. Percentages drop slightly for older generations, though a majority are friending and posting and liking alongside the Millennials. With nearly 2 billion active monthly users, Facebook is the social media king and your best bet for staying connected to patients, getting positive reviews, and reaching out to new patients.

Facebook has also taken an increasing interest in local service provider discovery, implementing several enhancements that improve the ability for users to easily find health care providers (and other local businesses). Facebook further offers outstanding demographic and location targeting via their paid advertising solutions, which allow practices to reach potential patients in their area for relatively low costs.

Of course, that means you need a Facebook page worth reading. When patients ask Facebook friends for health care recommendations and referrals, they're going to get links to numerous health care professionals' pages in response. If you want your page to capture their attention and convince them to call your office, you need to give them the information they want in an eye-catching, engaging way that fits the Facebook style.

Simply put, post valuable information and fun, engaging content and you'll have current and prospective patients lining up to like you.

INSTAGRAM

Instagram is one of the fastest growing social networks, thanks to its focus on stylish images and short videos. Immediately embraced by younger audiences (think college students posting photos of lattes or artists posting images of their work), Instagram was acquired by Facebook in 2012 and has since grown to be the second most popular social media network in the United States. Instagram already boasts more than 90 million users in the US alone, and it's projected that in 2017 more than half of all social media users will have an Instagram account they regularly use.

It has surpassed Twitter in user count and shames Facebook and Twitter when it comes to user engagement rates. Pew survey data indicates that 59 percent of Americans between the ages of 18 and 24 are already using Instagram, and older demographics are catching up.

Instagram depends on images and videos, so any medical or health care practice that has a cosmetic or physical element is a perfect fit for participating on the network. Dermatologists, dental and orthopedic providers, plastic surgeons, and others can use before and after pictures – or just the after's – to show prospective patients exactly what they can expect. When appropriate, encourage your patients to share pictures on their own Instagram accounts with a tag to your profile and/or link to your website, and you'll get the social media equivalent of a five-star referral.

TWITTER

Twitter is one of the least understood social networks. While not everyone can wrap their head around life in 140 characters, millions have, including your peers. This makes Twitter a must-use if you're looking to expand your network or raise your profile. It's also great to use when attending conferences or meetings, to either connect with other attendees or to share the event with your audience. The platform allows you to share stories and good news about your practice, ask questions and join conversations, and tweet about your own successes and insights in order to start boosting your professional esteem. If you want invitations to speak at gatherings and events or write-ups on local news sites, Twitter is your practice's best friend.

You can also find patients on Twitter, but don't expect a ton of appointment requests in your DMs. Since Twitter is most often used for consuming real-time news and commenting on one's fleeting life moments, it's not the first place patients go to find a medical provider.

Twitter does have a techier audience and is one of the few social networks to have more male than female users. The audience tends to be a bit younger as well, the majority of users being between the ages of 18 and 29. If for some reason your patients are younger, mostly male, and tech-savvy, you should definitely be on Twitter.

YOUTUBE

YouTube is not only an important social network (that's not always thought of as one), it's also the second largest search engine on the internet; the only other website that gets more searches is Google.

What really makes YouTube important, though, is the rising demand for video content online. This demand is so high that other social networks, including Facebook and Instagram, have begun giving display preference to videos in their news feeds. Online video is therefore the newest method of marketing your practice, and YouTube is the easiest place to do it.

Videos posted on YouTube can be embedded on your website and shared on social networks with the click of a button, both aiding in communicating the value your practice provides and documenting your professional expertise.

OTHER SOCIAL PLATFORMS

It seems like a new social network pops up every day, especially among young people. Expect this trend to continue for the foreseeable future.

One social network to pay particular attention to over the next few years is **Snapchat**. Snapchat has exploded in the past two years, growing in popularity with younger audiences who love to send disappearing pictures and videos. Few, if any, health care providers can claim they're successfully using the platform, so don't think you have to jump right in and start ripping selfies. If you're trying to reach a younger crowd of prospective patients with health tips and informal answers to general medical questions, though, this could be a useful tool in your health care office's online marketing arsenal.

Another social network you may find useful is **Doximity**. Built specifically for medical professionals (and students and residents) to keep in touch with each other and make new connections, Doximity is great for boosting your profile within your area of expertise and getting referrals from other local providers. This isn't the place for patient outreach, but if it's a bigger and stronger health care network you're looking for, Doximity is an easy way to get it.

Try experimenting with new social sites to see what works and what doesn't. New platforms are often the most valuable to users who get in early.

WHAT SHOULD I POST ON SOCIAL MEDIA?

Deciding what to post on your social media profiles depends, to a certain extent, on which platforms you are using. That being said, *your social media marketing should be working in sync across all of your profiles*, and therefore much of what you post will be very similar.

Each of your blog entries should be posted to your social media profiles, along with any new pages you add to your site. This can all be easily automated, too, so publishing your blog/new web pages automatically generates a Facebook post or a Tweet. Every post you put on Facebook (or anywhere else) should also include an image, whether it's an original photograph, a photo that you have a license to use (or that is free to use), a cartoon, or even a colorful (and easy to understand) chart, graph, or infographic.

Other ideas for images to post on social media include:

- Pictures of you with your happy, healing patients. When we see a picture of someone smiling, our brain lights up as if we're smiling ourselves. Pictures of you with patients looking confident, happy, healthy, relieved, or otherwise pleasant will inspire the same feelings in every prospective patient who sees your post. Make sure you get HIPAA waivers and permission to publicly share photos of your patients, of course!

- Funny selfies. Remember, you're the star of your practice and your social media. Patients want to see you, especially in a way that makes you seem approachable and engaging. Don't do anything that would undermine their confidence in you as a careful medical professional, but light-hearted selfies are the perfect way to show the human side of your health care practice.

- **Photos of your office and equipment.** Patients, or potential patients, often fear the unknown. Medical issues are always scary, in part because patients don't know what to expect. Show patients what they'll be treated to when they come in for a visit. New waiting room amenities, new equipment, new paintjobs – anytime you make a change, you have a few new photos to post to Instagram. You can also post pictures of the medical equipment you use, whether that's surgical instruments or the post-op braces a patient might expect to wear. Include a short description of what the piece of equipment is and how it works.

- **Pictures of the office staff.** Again, patients want to see the human side of your practice. Use social media as a chance to give them a preview of the friendly faces they'll meet when they come in for their appointment, and patients will be that much more likely to pick up the phone and get on your schedule.

- **Educational materials.** Use people's interest in learning more about their health and bodies to become a trusted authority. Share educational images, such as medical drawings, data graphics showing results from a relevant study, post-op recovery guidelines, or fascinating medical imagery (X-rays or infrared thermography) across your social media profiles to catch your patients' attention and establish your expertise.

- **Images from your other digital assets.** Do you have great photos of your practice, patients, and people on your website? Post them on Twitter or Facebook with a link back to your site. Repurposing images you've already created or bought for your blog posts, website, or advertising materials is a great way to promote more of your content.

- Inspirational quotes with compelling pictures. You don't have to get too cheesy, and you shouldn't make inspirational quotes the mainstay of your Instagram profile, but intermingling some of these with your other posts can help boost your reach, make patients feel confident and secure, and show them that you care about their well-being and state of mind even when they're not in the office.

Video content is also huge on social media, with some research finding that video posts on Facebook have a 135 percent higher organic reach than posts with photos. Short clips of you and your staff in the office or brief videos where you explain the basics of an illness, a preventative health care treatment, or a more advanced procedure are solid ways to start producing video content. Even videos of procedures themselves can be social media gold. YouTube users can subscribe to your practice's YouTube channel and even comment on the individual videos, providing opportunities for further engagement.

Finally, you can share media from other sources that provides relevant (and trustworthy!) health news and information. A couple quick clicks, and your Facebook page or Twitter profile will be populated with plenty of valuable insights from top-tier sources, intermingling with your own advice and images to give patients top-notch confidence in your skills.

GETTING THE MOST OUT OF SOCIAL MEDIA

Once you have decided which social media platforms make the most sense for your practice, how do you ensure that your time spent on these networks is achieving your desired results?

By now, you already know the basics of what you should be doing on social media: you need to create and publish novel posts to communicate your practice's mission and passions, share updates, provide educational content, interact with patients, and let your personality show through. This will engage your audience, especially when coupling your content with images, videos, and events they're interested in. There are further steps you can take, however, to bring your social media presence to the next level.

After crafting a mixture of posts that share different content, strategically arrange them in a marketing calendar. Be mindful of different variables that can influence engagement rates. For example, you shouldn't be posting dry pieces of content, such as peer-reviewed journal articles, on a frequent basis, unless you want your peers in for a visit. You can also experiment with different times of day to see if a particular window generates significantly higher patient engagement. If your audience is most receptive on Wednesday evenings, maybe this would be a good time to share a product, service, or promotion you're trying to push. By experimenting with your content, examining the metrics, and honing your strategy, your marketing can make a bigger impact with patients.

Social media also facilitates communication with current and future patients. They may reach out to ask questions about the practice (if they're not yet a patient), to thank you for your help with their condition, or even to confirm their appointment. The key to this engagement is simply to

140

make sure someone responds to them in a timely manner. All too often, patients or customers reach out to a doctor or brand via social media, and their comment or message is never addressed. *Responding to a patient makes them feel more like a person*, rather than a number, which builds rapport and establishes a closer relationship between your patients and your practice. Properly using social media channels in this way can be time consuming, but there are ways to streamline your efforts.

One tactic to reduce your time commitment is to take larger sources of content, like a detailed guide or a book, and divide them into smaller pieces to use as blog content; this repurposed material can then also be shared on social media, saving you time you may not have to spend. Share these posts, and then link to the full-length article on your blog, website, or third-party source.

Another way to more efficiently use your time is to spend a few hours writing all of your social media content for the month. This way, you're writing consistently across all channels, and can better strategize when you want to share certain information. You can also use a social network aggregation tool like Hootsuite, Sprout Social, or Buffer to schedule posts ahead of time for all your social media channels. This cuts down on posting times and alerts you whenever someone interacts with a post or tweet. The time you save on crafting social media content can then be put to good use elsewhere.

Finally, social media is an inexpensive way to advertise your practice. Many of the most popular social media platforms have different advertising opportunities, and campaign setup is easy if you know what you're doing. Facebook and Instagram let you target ads based on demographics, interest, and geography with incredible precision. Social advertising also helps bolster practice name recognition and improve the return on investment (ROI) of your overall efforts. This topic will be addressed in greater depth in the next chapter.

SOCIAL MEDIA AND HIPAA

Many health care providers wonder what implications the Health Insurance Portability and Accountability Act (HIPAA) has for social media. In a day and age where one false step could land a malpractice lawsuit on your desk, it's important to remember that social media is happening in a public forum.

Social media is like any other aspect of your field when it comes to social media: use common sense and apply the "Coffee Shop Test." Before you post anything on social media, consider: would discussing this information over coffee with a friend or colleague be a HIPAA violation? If so, then social media isn't the place to publicize it.

Overall, make sure to avoid discussing or posting the Protected Health Information (PHI) of a patient anywhere online. Keep it out of your posts, and be cautious with the personal messaging features on your chosen social media platforms. Unless you're sure the platform is secure and the information won't land in the wrong hands, it might be best to communicate with your patients via email or telephone if sensitive personal information might come up in the conversation. If for some reason you plan to use a patient's information, likeness, name, or story in any content you publish online, make sure you get his or her permission through a written patient consent form first.

Your practice can't ignore social media, not if you want to keep up with the changing ways in which patients find, evaluate and decide upon a provider for care. Social platforms can be used as effective tools for educating patients, engaging them in conversation, and for augmenting outbound communications and brand awareness. Social media is the new – and improved – word-of-mouth marketing.

MASTERING SOCIAL MEDIA CHECKLIST:

- ☐ Have a clear social media strategy, and have a purpose for each social media channel where your medical practice has a profile.

- ☐ Identify which social media platforms will be the most beneficial to your practice.

- ☐ Join these platforms and claim your practice's profile on them.

- ☐ Optimize your practice's profile on each site; at a minimum, this means having a quality profile image, clear contact information, and a link to your practice website.

- ☐ Create a social media content posting schedule.

- ☐ Post to social media accounts, and participate in conversations.

- ☐ Continuously monitor each practice's social media profiles.

- ☐ Get trend metrics from your current posts on each social media site. Use these as your baseline metrics for comparing and refining your future posting strategies.

- ☐ Create paid social media advertising campaigns for each practice.

- ☐ Monitor campaign performance for each practice profile to see what works.

- ☐ Iterate campaigns to continually improve performance, using quantitative data.

CHAPTER 10

ADVERTISING YOUR PRACTICE ONLINE

We've talked a lot about SEO, content marketing, and social media, and each of these plays a huge role in marketing your medical practice. Your inbound marketing strategy wouldn't be complete, however, without paid advertising.

Doctors typically advertise in traditional forms of media (TV, radio, print, and billboards) because that's what they're used to. In many major cities, large hospitals and practices consistently promote themselves through these channels. These mediums are no longer the first choice for savvy marketers, however, and for good reason - *the return on investment (ROI) from traditional media is often less than what could be achieved by spending advertising dollars online.* When's the last time you received quantifiable metrics reporting on how many people your 30-second radio spot brought into your practice? Do you have any idea which advertising platforms are working for you, and to what extent they're benefitting your practice?

Best practices suggest an internal audit of your current advertising efforts to see where to allocate your limited practice marketing dollars. If your practice is getting good results with traditional mediums, don't abandon them. However, you should also try incorporating paid search engine and social media advertising into these efforts. Combining traditional advertising campaigns with your digital advertising is ideal – all your advertising channels should work collaboratively toward the common goal of getting your practice new patients.

Even if your practice is not engaging in offline advertising campaigns, paid search and social advertising can complement your SEO and content creation efforts, capitalize where your business is strongest, or supplement an underperforming area of your practice's marketing.

WHAT IS PPC ADVERTISING?

PPC stands for pay-per-click, and is sometimes referred to as paid search, when speaking about search engine PPC advertising. When you buy PPC online advertisements, you pay a small fee each time a patient clicks on your ad. There are other paid advertising models like CPM, or cost-per-mille (thousand) advertising, where you pay based on the number of times your ad appears – this is how newspaper, radio, and TV advertisements are sold. PPC is a much better model because you only pay for an action (a click), not a non-action (a view). PPC advertising is a key component in jump-starting web traffic and increasing patient volume for many medical practices.

Both search engines and social networks offer PPC advertising, but each of them differs in terms of cost and effectiveness. For instance, if they're done right, Google ads will drive high volumes of traffic to your site, but can be more expensive than advertising on other search engines. Bing, on the other hand, is often less expensive than Google, but it's also less popular, so you may not see as much traffic and thus will attract fewer new appointments. Social networks like Facebook often have lower click-through rates than search engines, but the targeting capabilities offered by social media platforms still make them highly effective. They are also extremely low-cost; with a budget of just a few hundred dollars, you can effectively drive engagement with potential patients and raise awareness of your practice.

You should view social media and search engine advertising as complementary to each other (and to your other internet marketing efforts), since both have different purposes and outcomes. Social media users, for instance, aren't intentionally searching for you or your services, but they will see your ads as they browse their news streams. *The best social ads don't really look like ads* – your ads might feature an interesting blog post, a useful download, or a video about a medical condition. Remember, patients on social networks are there to chat with friends and family, not to book a provider. They might not become patients immediately, but your ads will raise their awareness of your practice, and when they do need a health care provider, they'll know who to call.

Search engine users, on the other hand, will see your ads when they enter specific search terms related to your practice. Since they are intentionally looking for you, the conditions you treat, or the services you provide, you will see a higher click-through rate and more immediate conversion of this traffic into new patient appointments. Paying for ads also helps you appear at the top of search results, since Google and other search engines show paid advertisements before their local and organic listings.

This makes search engine PPC advertising a great way to kick-start your online efforts and drive immediate new patient appointments, while you wait for your SEO efforts to drive your local and organic rankings.

WHY SHOULD HEALTH CARE PRACTICES USE PPC ADVERTISING?

You may wonder why your health care practice should use PPC when you've already got a good SEO strategy going for you.

At InboundMD, we believe that PPC and SEO work hand-in-hand. SEO is great because it gives you a broad reach. PPC complements that broad reach by attracting specific patients. SEO is also a long-term strategy that can take months to produce visible results. Good PPC ads, however, are live instantly and will immediately start sending traffic to your site, allowing you to quickly and efficiently reach prospective patients in need of your medical services on search engines like Google, Yahoo, and Bing.

Another reason to use PPC advertising is that even with a strong SEO strategy, you're not always going to be in Google's local 3-pack or at the top of search results. Paid ads will always appear before any other results, however, because you paid for that spot; you'll be the first thing patients see.

PPC ads, even at their most basic level, also allow you to target patients within a particular geographic area; paid social media advertising allows for even more specific demographic targeting.

DEVELOPING A PPC ADVERTISING STRATEGY FOR YOUR PRACTICE

ESTABLISH GOALS

Why are you advertising in the first place? Are you interested in getting more new patients, or do you just want to raise awareness for a new clinic that you've recently opened? The first step in creating an effective PPC advertising strategy is to determine your goals. It sounds simple, but many practices forget to do this before they start advertising, and their campaigns usually fail because of it.

Regardless of the goals you have for your practice advertising, make sure that they are SMART: Specific, Measurable, Agreed-upon, Realistic, and Trackable.

SETTING A BUDGET

The next step in getting your PPC campaign started is to determine your budget. If you don't take time to work through this step carefully, you could end up spending much more than you intended to. Various tools like the bid simulators built into Google AdWords can help you refine your budget and estimate how your ads will perform at particular dollar amounts.

We recommend most providers start with at least $1,000 per month. If that is more than your practice can currently afford, you may want to focus on the other aspects of internet marketing for the time being, especially listings management and SEO.

CHOOSE SEARCH ENGINE OR SOCIAL MEDIA ADVERTISING

Deciding whether to focus your PPC campaign on a search engine or on social media depends on the goals you have for your practice. You can start with both (and we're sure some practices do this), but you might find it easier to begin by selecting one search engine or social network that you feel can best help you achieve your goals.

For example, if you're looking for new patient appointments right away, targeting patients searching on Google is the best place to start. If you're looking to grow your patient audience and engage with patients more frequently after they visit, social advertising is probably the better option.

Either way, start small and experiment often.

DETERMINE AN OFFER

There needs to be a reason for a patient to interact with your ad. This doesn't mean that you need to offer a coupon or a discount, but you do need to have something that the patient wants.

In most cases, what you have is the solution to a prospective patient's health or medical condition, which is more than enough to offer. The

151

majority of your ad creative, therefore, regardless of the medium, should focus on selling your experience and the results you can provide, and not necessarily the prices you charge. If you're using social media ads to market your practice, your offer will likely be a piece of content or information that patients would enjoy.

Always remember that there is competition in your area, and patients can be swayed by enticing offers from health care providers.

DEVELOP CREATIVE

Armed with an offer, you can now develop the ad campaign creative – the copy (and in some cases imagery) that will drive patient action.

Your copy should be all about your patients. Copy that focuses on you or your practice won't attract patients as effectively as copy that tells them what they'll get by choosing your practice. Ask yourself what you can give your patients that will set you apart from your competition.

For instance, an ad that reads, "Prestigious Orthopedic Surgeon. State-of-the-Art Office and Location" will do nothing for the patient. Quality advertising tells patients about all the good things a provider has to offer them. For example, a good ad might communicate to patients that when they make an appointment they will receive best-in-class treatment, that their treatment will be customized to their needs, not one-size-fits-all, and that they don't need to go through a confusing referral process just to get an appointment.

PPC ADVERTISING FOR SEARCH ENGINES

There are some aspects of PPC advertising that are unique to either search engines or social media, and you should make sure to craft your PPC campaign strategy accordingly.

CHOOSING YOUR KEYWORDS

For search engine campaigns, your PPC ads are limited to text and links. This means that choosing the right search terms to have your ads show against is crucial. Again, like your budget, this should be a thoughtful process. Patients are going online to search for information on their condition before treatment, and often before they even set foot inside of a practice location. They are searching for their specific condition as well as generalized terms, like "{location} knee pain." These are the terms you want your advertising to target in order to get the potential patient's attention while his or her issue is top-of-mind. This is also something that traditional mediums of advertising, like billboards, simply cannot do. Google Keyword Planner, as discussed in Chapter 4, can help you find search terms relevant to your medical practice and suggest bid rates for them.

Take "hand surgery" as a search term, for example. "Hand surgery" is a somewhat competitive term, and Google suggests a fairly high bid for advertising to appear when it is searched. Other terms, like "hand doctor" and "carpal tunnel syndrome," are also expensive. Terms like "carpal tunnel relief" or "carpal tunnel treatment," however, have lower monthly searches but are much less expensive. Try to choose a few of the more popular search terms as well as some of the less common ones for a balanced ad campaign.

Over time, it's important to refine your keywords. It may seem easier to just let your campaign run by itself, but to achieve the best results you'll want to constantly update your search terms, getting rid of those that aren't working and adding new terms that might be more profitable. You may also want to add negative keywords, those that you do not want your advertisements to appear against, to help improve the effectiveness of your ads.

GEO-TARGETING AND LOCAL SEARCH

Once you've determined your keywords, it's time to narrow down who sees your ads. For instance, if you practice in Albany, New York, you don't want patients in Miami, Florida clicking on your ads and costing you money when they will probably never visit your office.

To do this in Google AdWords, select your campaign, open "Settings," and navigate down to the "Location" section. In the search field you can select areas you wish to target as well as regions you would like to exclude from your targeting.

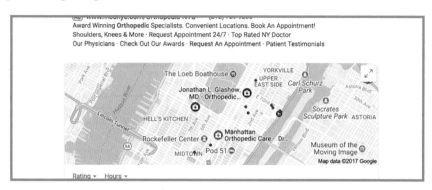

You can also target languages. For example, if your city has a high Korean population, you can include ads in Korean to reach that demographic. Search engines will not translate ads for you, however, so make sure your ads are already written in the language you are targeting.

PPC ADVERTISING FOR SOCIAL NETWORKS

In most ways, PPC advertising on social media is similar to PPC advertising on search engines. The key differences between social media ads and search engine ads lie in the types of targeting you can perform and the varieties of ad creative you can develop.

ENHANCED DEMOGRAPHIC TARGETING

Social networks offer different advertising targeting options than search engines. Social media platforms come with powerful tools that allow you to target a very specific set of patient demographics, thereby choosing exactly who sees your ad. You can target patients based on their age, gender, language, relationships, work, interests, life events, behaviors, and more. As with search engine PPC advertising, you can target your local area, but social media also allows you to advertise directly to particular groups within that area.

For instance, if your practice specializes in knee surgery on older patients, your social media ads should be targeted to middle-aged and elderly social media users in your practice area. On the other hand, if you focus more on sports injury treatment, you'll want to target a younger demographic, perhaps twenty to forty-year-olds who are interested in running.

ENGAGING AD CREATIVE

Another difference between social advertising and search engine advertising is the type of ad creative you can use.

With search engine advertising, you are restricted to creating text-only advertisements. Social advertising allows you to use pictures and videos, alongside text, to produce engaging and interactive ads. In some cases, you can even show multiple images or videos, to showcase more than one message about your clinic or treatment you provide. This gives you a lot more flexibility and power over how you convey your value to patients.

Regardless of the platform, it's important to have multiple versions of your ads running at the same time. While you don't have to test huge variations, you should always be trying to find a better advertisement that converts more viewers into patients. Plus, if you're experimenting with a new demographic or a new set of keywords, getting data back on multiple different ads can help you make decisions on future campaign tweaks. You should also be rotating ads at least every month in conjunction with changing offers, unless you've found something that consistently works.

IMPLEMENT TRACKING

Search engine and social media advertising platforms provide practices with in-depth tracking capabilities, which allow you to measure and track how your ads are performing. In order to best track a PPC advertising campaign, you will also need to have analytics on your website, so you can identify which advertisements are generating the most new patient appointments. You'll also want to leverage call tracking, as not all patients book appointments online. While many online tools exist to track the various movements of patients, your front office staff will need to bear some responsibility for this, as well. Updating patient forms to include your online advertising campaigns in the "How did you hear about us?" section will greatly help in making sure you know what approaches are working best.

Many medical and health care practices have never considered advertising – offline or online. This presents a tremendous opportunity for those practices that advertise effectively, especially online, to get ahead of their competition. With the ability to target specific patients and track what's working and what's not, paid online advertising should absolutely be added to your internet marketing arsenal, especially if you've already got the basics of traditional advertising covered.

ADVERTISING YOUR PRACTICE ONLINE CHECKLIST:

- ☐ Conduct an internal audit of your current advertising efforts.
- ☐ Determine which channels are providing the best and worst ROI.
- ☐ Determine who you want to target with your advertising, including their demographics and geographic locations.
- ☐ Set a budget for your advertising efforts, and define what offer will set you apart from your competition.
- ☐ Decide whether search engine advertising or social media advertising makes more sense for your practice.
- ☐ Create ad positioning and copy that resonates with your target patients.
- ☐ Leverage the power of Google, Yahoo, and Bing by creating PPC ads.
- ☐ Create targeted ads on social networks, particularly Facebook.
- ☐ Use targeting programs to aim your ads at your target demographics.
- ☐ Run multiple versions of an ad at once, to determine whether one version proves more successful than another.
- ☐ Integrate improved tracking to measure campaign effectiveness.
- ☐ Examine each campaign's metrics and analytics to iterate and fine-tune them over time.

CHAPTER 11

REFINING YOUR PROCESS THROUGH TRACKING AND ANALYTICS

The final (and most important) piece of a successful practice marketing campaign is tracking and iterating your marketing efforts using quantitative data found through the use of online analytics.

Online analytics is the silver bullet of the internet marketing world. Online analytics – among other things – gives you the ability to measure campaign performance using specific metrics.

Unlike traditional advertising, such as print and radio, internet marketing provides you with a huge amount of data; this data will then allow you to draw conclusions about which of your marketing strategies or campaigns are giving you the greatest results. From phone numbers to clicks, almost every aspect of an inbound practice marketing campaign can be tracked and reported upon. *Through website, search, social, and email analytics, you will be able to see what's working and what's not.*

WHAT IS ONLINE ANALYTICS?

Online analytics is software installed on your website that enables the monitoring and reporting of website usage as data points for the purposes of understanding and improving the way the website attracts, converts, and keeps customers.

The underlying principle behind online analytics is that if you can track, monitor, and report on enough data you can gain continuous insights into how to best improve one's site performance – and how to attract and delight patients.

Most online analytics programs are enabled by placing a piece of JavaScript on the pages of a website, allowing the program to collect certain data about how patients got to the website, what actions they took once they arrived, and what prompted them to leave.

WHY USE ONLINE ANALYTICS?

The reason online analytics should be used as part of your practice's internet marketing strategy is fairly self-explanatory. Fundamentally, you should use online analytics to gain a greater understanding of your patients and how they use your website, as well as to get insight into which of your marketing campaigns are working the best. It also allows you to identify and take advantage of opportunities that you may not have otherwise known about.

More specifically, you should employ online analytics because it allows you to:

- **Measure Practice Reach**–Online analytics allow you to measure your presence and website's overall reach. "Reach" is defined as the number of users who are exposed to your campaign advertisement, or, at a more basic level, your website. Measuring reach is important because "reaching" more people on the internet is one way of increasing patients. Seeing an increase in reach is a sign of positive growth for your practice's marketing effort.

- **Measure Patient Acquisition**–It's not enough to simply measure how many potential patients you are reaching with your marketing, you need to know how many patients you're actually acquiring – and how much it costs to acquire them. Measuring acquisition and the costs that are associated with each conversion is important as these are the only variables in a campaign that can always be controlled. Additionally, knowing your acquisition costs allows you to determine which campaigns are the most popular and therefore which campaigns should receive more (or less) of your marketing budget.

- **Measure Conversion**–Successful campaigns are about more than just getting patients to your site. You also need to get them to make an appointment online or call your practice. Measuring conversions tells you what percentage of your website's traffic converts to appointments or other actions you can track. These are important data points because the metrics surrounding them will show you what needs to be improved in order to deliver more patients to your practice. Remember: you want to get lots of traffic and know where it's coming from and how much it's costing you, but you also want to know which marketing campaign is converting best!

- **Measure Retention**–You spend a lot of money in an attempt to acquire patients. But once they've seen you once, do they come back? Repeat visits are crucial to being successful for many specialties. In general, most existing patients convert at a far higher rate than new patients, and the more existing patients use your services, the less they end up costing you to acquire in the long run. Measuring retention will allow you to identify areas of improvement in operations to keep existing patients coming back to your practice.

With online analytics you can pretty much track, monitor, and report on everything related to your site. That makes using online analytics a must in today's highly competitive environment.

ONLINE ANALYTICS TERMINOLOGY

The following terminology is widely used and necessary to understand in order to successfully utilize an online analytics program.

- **Pageview**–The number of times a certain page is viewed by a website visitor. This metric can also be used to describe the total number of pageviews a website receives.

- **Unique Visit**–A unique instance of an individual arriving at a website page. This metric can also be used to describe the total number of individuals arriving at a website in its entirety.

- **Keyword**–A keyword is the word or phrase that a user searches to find your website or web page.

- **Referrer**–A referrer is a source of user traffic to a website or webpage.

- **Conversion Rate**–The percentage of unique visitors to a site that take a particular action. This action could be to consummate a sale, fill out a form, download something, etc.

- **Abandonment Rate**–Abandonment rate is the measure of the number or percentage of people who drop out of a certain online process. Abandonment rate is most frequently discussed when talking about the online scheduling process, but could also refer to things such as the email sign-up process or, if you were selling a product on your website, the checkout process. The abandonment rate would measure the number of patients who began one of these processes but failed to complete it.

- **Bounce Rate**–Bounce rate represents the percentage of initial visitors to a site who "bounce" away to a different site, rather than continue on to other pages within the same site. Bounce rate is typically used to determine things like the engagement or "stickiness" of a site.

- **Segmentation**–Segmentation is the identification, labeling or filtering of a subset of a website's traffic, users, or buyers based on similar trends, actions, or habits.

- **Frequency**–Frequency is the number of times a person visits a website. Frequency could also be used to measure the number of times a customer makes a purchase.

- **Recency**–Recency refers to the period between the last and current visit of a website user. This metric is often used to gauge the effectiveness of a campaign's ability to increase visitor loyalty.

ONLINE ANALYTICS TOOLS

As you've read above, online analytics software comes with a number of ways to get to better know your customers, monitor your campaigns, and measure transactions. Below, you will find an overview of three online analytics tools (common reports and filters) that are frequently used to accomplish these aims.

Visitor Segmentation Tools–Visitor segmentation allows you to group or break down your total traffic by a common factor. By default, most analytics programs group traffic by referrer, but with segmentation you can group total traffic (or traffic by referrer) by things such as geographic area, time on site, amount of purchase, frequency of purchase, etc. Armed with this information, you will be in a better position to understand which traffic streams and website users you should focus on.

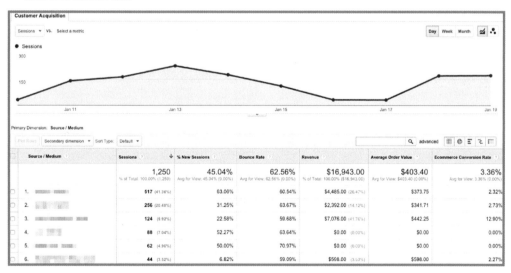

Campaign Analysis Tools–Using URL appending codes, goals, filters, and canned reports, one can set up and monitor campaigns in almost real time. This gives you insights into the leverage points that can be used to make improvements to campaigns to increase ROI and overall success. In addition, campaign analysis tools will allow you to identify patterns and opportunities that could not be gleaned otherwise.

Commerce Measurement Tools–The most powerful and frequently used of all online analytics tools are those that allow for commerce measurement. Commerce measurement tools allow you to track and measure conversions, overall sales, sales by channel/referrer/segment, shopping cart abandonment rate, and conversion rate. These commerce measurement tools will give you much of the information you need to report on the success – or failure – of your campaigns.

IMPLEMENTING AND SETTING UP YOUR ONLINE ANALYTICS

In order to implement online analytics software and begin tracking your campaigns and website performance, you will not only need the technical knowledge of how to update your website, but also the proper access to make such updates.

If this technical knowledge is outside of your wheelhouse, don't worry. Your IT person, webmaster, or marketing agency should be able to implement all of this for you. Even if you think you can do it yourself, it might still be best to leave installation to the experts – after all, you want to make sure that you're getting the right data. This will only happen if the tracking codes are set up properly.

Once you have implemented your online analytics tracking code, you will need to program the analytics software to track and report on the metrics and areas of interests that you've decided to use to determine campaign success.

Since there are a number of different online analytics programs with specific features and functions, what follows is a basic overview of the most important steps to take when getting started with your online analytics set-up.

- Determine which actions you want to track. Most online analytics programs provide you with the prerequisite metrics necessary to judge campaign success, but they don't necessarily track the specific actions – a button clicked, a phone number dialed, or a form submitted – that are key to understanding the overall performance and results of your marketing campaigns. Establishing a list of the actions you want to track on your website or landing page is the first step in setting up your analytics.

· **Implement campaign tracking code.** In order to determine the effectiveness of your off-site advertising or marketing efforts, and the actions that occur as a result of them, you will want to set up tracking codes for each of your campaigns within your online analytics program. This tracking could take the form of a string of parameters that are appended to a link placed in a post on a third party website, or additional code applied to parts of your own website. You may need to do this frequently, especially if you're launching new campaigns with regularity.

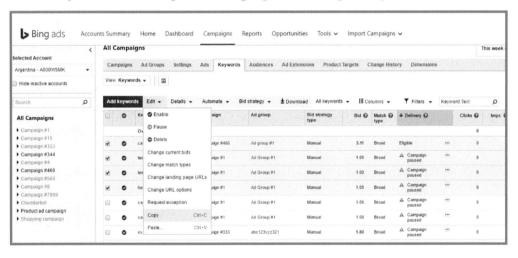

· **Create and automate reporting.** The final part of your online analytics set-up addresses the part you likely care the most about – seeing the data behind your marketing efforts, and not having to log in to the analytics software in order to do so. Through your online analytics program, you can configure specific reports and automate their delivery via email, precisely when you want them. Trust me when I say that you don't want to be logging in to your analytics software with any frequency – it can easily become a time suck that will fascinate you, but not help you grow your practice. It's best to create the reports you need and have them automatically sent to you.

Data without action, however, is worthless. In order to leverage this data, you must draw conclusions and make iterations when necessary. Strategies such as A/B testing will provide previously hidden insight and allow you to make adjustments to ensure campaign success.

This means that as you progress through marketing campaigns for your practice, you can quickly pivot and eliminate underperforming strategies that may have initially sounded good, but were proven ineffective. You can then invest this time and money into strategies which are working and bringing new patients to your practice.

Remember, Coca-Cola and Pepsi spend billions every year on marketing, despite being household names. Marketing your practice is not a one-time thing or a route to quick success; it's an all-the-time thing that, if done right, gets more effective the more it is used.

REFINING YOUR PROCESS: TRACKING AND ANALYTICS CHECKLIST:

- ☐ Create a website analytics account for your practice.
- ☐ Determine which actions you are most interested in tracking.
- ☐ Implement analytics code on your practice website(s).
- ☐ Set up website analytics reports for your practice website(s).
- ☐ Iterate website design and advertising campaigns based on analytical results.
- ☐ Create a social media analytics account for each practice account.
- ☐ Implement social media analytics code on each practice's social media profile(s).
- ☐ Set up social media analytics reports for each practice account.
- ☐ Iterate social media strategies based on initial results.
- ☐ Set up email analytics reports.
- ☐ Review email analytics reports.
- ☐ Iterate email marketing strategies based on results.

CHAPTER 12

INTERNET MARKETING AND HIPAA COMPLIANCE

Prior to the Health Insurance Portability and Accountability Act of 1996 (HIPAA), no general requirements for protecting health information existed in the health care industry. With the development and widespread adoption of electronic health records and computerized systems, however, an increase in the risk of exposure of confidential patient health information drove policy-makers to take action.

The goal of HIPAA is to protect the privacy of the protected health information (PHI) a practice receives, maintains, or transmits. This security rule requires medical practices to maintain "reasonable and appropriate" administrative, technical, and physical safeguards for protecting PHI. This includes security management processes that identify and analyze potential risks, designated security personnel to safeguard protected information, properly managed PHI access, workforce training, and the performance of periodic self-evaluations.

HIPAA also calls for physical and technical safeguards, including strict facility access and control guidelines, and mandates that PHI not be incorrectly altered or destroyed. Business associates, such as your marketing team, must sign a written business agreement that specifically establishes what they have been engaged to do; HIPAA compliance is then required of these associates, as well.

With regards to marketing, HIPAA compliance means never revealing PHI, either directly or indirectly. For example, if you were to email a group of diabetes patients about a new tool to help monitor blood glucose levels, it would be a HIPAA violation if the email address bar publicly displayed the identities of each individual recipient. Compliance with the law also means never selling PHI to third parties. In general, if someone could make an inference about a patient's health based on the marketing material you have sent to them, you are likely violating HIPAA.

A communication is not considered marketing if it is "made for treatment of the individual," according to the U.S. Department of Health & Human Services – for example, when a health care provider mails prescription refill reminders to patients. However, it's best not to play too closely to the rules of what's allowed by HIPAA; always err on the side of caution.

It's important to point out that the HIPAA information contained in this chapter is not legal advice, as I am not a lawyer. To learn more about HIPAA compliance, please talk to your legal counsel, and read the useful information on the U.S. Department of Health & Human Services website, www.HHS.gov.

INTERNET MARKETING AND HIPPA COMPLIANCE CHECKLIST:

- ☐ Create and maintain "reasonable and appropriate" administrative safeguards, including workforce training.
- ☐ Create and maintain "reasonable and appropriate" technical safeguards, including managing PHI access.
- ☐ Create and maintain "reasonable and appropriate" physical safeguards, including regulating facility and computer access.
- ☐ Identify and analyze potential risks within your practice.
- ☐ Conduct a periodic self-evaluation of proper PHI protocol.
- ☐ Require written business agreements with business associates who have access to PHI.
- ☐ Ensure practice marketing strategies don't violate HIPAA rules.
- ☐ Ask legal counsel for clarification whenever unsure of HIPAA rules.

TYING IT ALL TOGETHER

As you've seen, being an excellent practitioner in your field is no longer enough to generate and retain patients; you must have excellent practice marketing, as well. And, well, it's pretty complicated with all of the moving parts and pieces.

Now it's time to tie it all together and formulate a game plan for the development of your practice's internet marketing efforts. It's something we use at InboundMD with practices across the country to improve their online visibility.

As you can see, we have broken the work up into digestible chunks for you – this helps maintain your momentum once you get started. Follow this step-by-step guide to know where you should prioritize your efforts and when objectives should ideally be accomplished. It also assumes you've never planned or executed on a marketing campaign in the past; if you have, your timeline may look somewhat different.

MONTH 1: BENCHMARKS AND PLANNING

During the first month, you should take time to step outside of your practice and understand where you presently stand. Consider this your initial check-up. You should strive to assess your current marketing efforts and online presence, establish basic benchmarks, develop your goals, and create a marketing plan to use as a roadmap during your practice marketing efforts.

1. Research and document your current state of marketing, including performance and any other available metrics.

2. Define the goals for your practice marketing (over whatever period for which you're planning) and identify the performance

metrics you will need to measure to monitor your progress toward achieving these goals.

3. Conduct a thorough audit of your website, search rankings, directory listings, review site profiles, and social media accounts.

4. Perform internal, keyword, industry, and competitive research to hone in on opportunities and targets for your campaigns.

5. Create target Patient Personas, tying them to popular keywords and your current service offerings and treatments.

6. Develop your overall practice marketing plan, complete with channel-specific strategies, and identify the steps you must take to implement it.

MONTHS 2 AND 3: IMPLEMENTATION AND OPTIMIZATION

After your roadmap is complete, it's time to start putting the building blocks of your marketing efforts into place. This starts with setting up tracking and analytics programs to ensure that your marketing efforts are being as effective as possible. Once this has been completed, you'll want to move toward updating your website with any missing calls-to-action, as well as implementing any required optimizations to improve your search visibility.

1. Implement your appointment reminder and post-visit review or survey software.

2. Determine actions and events to track on your website to monitor marketing campaign results.

3. Implement your online analytics tracking code on website and links used in ads.

4. Create and automate your online analytics reporting for your website as well as for your email and social media campaigns.

5. Set up your website with Google Search Console and ensure that there are no errors or warnings.

6. Optimize your existing website and content based on the keywords selected during the research you conducted in Month 1.

7. Set up and begin monitoring your keyword rankings in search engines.

MONTHS 4 AND 5: SEARCH AND SOCIAL

With your internet marketing infrastructure in place, you can now start implementing the marketing channels and campaigns required to be successful today, starting with off-site search engine optimization, online reputation management, and social media. Your Google My Business profile should be claimed and optimized alongside your major review website profiles. Social media profiles should be audited and/or claimed prior to the creation of specific social media assets for use in monthly campaigns.

1. Find, claim, and optimize your Google My Business profile.

2. Find, claim, and optimize your online review website profiles.

3. Set up your online rating and review monitoring software.

4. Begin creating missing pages and content on your website to target patient keyword searches.

5. Audit and/or create your social media profiles, updating design elements and adding images, videos, and text content in line with your marketing efforts.

6. Determine applicable outlets to begin link building efforts.

MONTH 6: LISTINGS MANAGEMENT

Now that you're half-way through a 12-month marketing campaign cycle, there's one more piece to put in place before your monthly efforts can become more routine. This remaining piece – your business and medical directory listings – will take an entire month for you to address, however, even if you're doing it with the help of software or an outside agency. Despite this heavy focus on your listings, don't take your eyes off of your analytics and reporting – you should constantly be seeing results and gaining insights on how you can further improve.

1. Find, claim, and optimize your business and medical directory listings.

2. Continue the creation of required content for missing pages on your website.

3. Monitor keyword rankings for each keyword phrase you're targeting.

4. Monitor incoming reviews, soliciting positive ratings from satisfied patients.

5. Create and publish social media posts that promote the practice and the content you're creating.

MONTHS 7 AND BEYOND: ADJUSTMENTS AND ONGOING MAINTENANCE

By month seven, everything should now be in place to begin the standardized marketing of your practice. This process of tracking progress, making alterations, testing new strategies, and optimizing existing campaigns will continue to build your patient acquisition, ensure a consistent level of new inbound patients, protect your online reputation, and build your practice's digital medical library. Additionally, at this time you can begin exploring brand expansion through advertising, email, and video content.

1. Review first six months' efforts, evaluating results and metrics.

2. Adjust and further hone your marketing plan and strategies based on the findings.

3. Monitor keyword rankings for each keyword phrase you're targeting.

4. Monitor incoming reviews, soliciting positive ratings from satisfied patients.

5. Continue the creation of required content for missing pages on your website.

6. Create and publish social media posts that promote the practice and the content you're creating.

7. Determine readiness and budget to begin PPC and/or social media advertising.

8. Begin cross-promoting your efforts between marketing channels so they work in concert with one other.

9. Select and set up email marketing software, with plans to begin regularly sending newsletters to your patients.

You've done it! Your inbound practice marketing is now on the right track.

At this point, you must continue to write (or have someone write for you) new content every day (social), week (blog), and month (newsletter). Additionally, analyze your performance metrics on a regular basis so you can adjust your strategy as necessary.

This will allow you to continually improve your online presence, which inevitably leads to more awareness and, of course, new patients.

WHERE TO GO FROM HERE

This is just the beginning of your practice marketing efforts online. While this book presents a fairly comprehensive overview of the best practices for successfully marketing your practice online, it's not specific to any one specialty or set of practice goals.

It's important that you take time to digest the information you've just consumed and use it to formulate a plan that is customized to fit your particular specialty and goals. It's also important to determine whether you want to go it alone or enlist the services of a consultant or agency to handle your practice marketing efforts for you.

Remember, the internet landscape is always changing. During the editing of this book, Google announced two new updates to their algorithm. This blistering rate of change produces new challenges and opportunities on a monthly basis, and it takes time and effort for any online marketing strategy to keep up. Successful internet marketing does not happen with one single event or campaign, but through consistent execution over time.

Of course, that's why InboundMD exists. We have the knowledge and tools necessary to make internet marketing work for your practice, and to execute on campaigns that will achieve your goals. Should you wish to discuss your practice's needs with InboundMD, give us a call at 1-800-818-7199, email garrett@InboundMD.com, or visit www.inboundmd.com to schedule a time to speak.

Thank you for taking the time to read through this book. I hope you've found it educational and inspirational, and I wish you the best of luck with your practice marketing efforts!

Made in the USA
Monee, IL
04 September 2019